EX LIBRIS
SOUTH ORANGE
PUBLIC LIBRARY

The Australians

Produced and
Photographed by
Robert B. Goodman

Text by
George Johnston

Designed by
Harry Williamson

Edited by
Jonathan Rinehart

Rigby Limited

The Australians

Rigby Limited, James Place, Adelaide
Sydney, Melbourne, Brisbane, Perth

First published September 1966

Second edition March 1967

Library of Congress Catalog Card
Number 66-21204

Printed and bound in Australia at
The Griffin Press, Adelaide
Six colour and two colour separations
and lithographic plates by
Ralfs and Hermsdorf, Sydney
Progressive proofs by
S. & A. Wheeler, Sydney
Set in 12 point Monophoto Bembo
by D. W. Paterson Co., Prahran, Victoria
with Univers series 689 and 693

Photographic colour processing and
printing for reproduction by
Group Color Pty Limited, Sydney
and Denny C. Harris Inc., Cleveland, Ohio
Black and white photographic prints for
reproduction by George Martin,
Meridian Photographics, New York City

Registered in Australia for
transmission by post as a book

To my parents, and to Barbara

Contents

The Land

It was never really intended as a place for people.

No ape ever walked upright in Australia's thickets and savannas, no tarsier or lemur chattered in its trees, no half-man in the first light of humanity's awakening crouched watchful in his middens. The great land slept on in its southern seas, while on all the other continents the human race developed and spread and made its artifacts and began its ceremonies. Bone had been carved and needles made and the cave walls of Lascaux and Altamira magically painted before any man ever trod the earth of the southern continent.

All that is Australia begins not with man but with the land itself; and all the dramas of today's Australia are played in the eternal presence of ancient beginnings, which is the land.

Lodged within spacious oceans beneath a tiara of archipelagoes and scattered islands, Australia looks on a map the way a continent ought to look, like a fruit ought to taste like a peach or an apple. It has the quality, too, of absorbing a multitude of characters from its surroundings – the long run of empty oceanic distances, the spicy aromatic tang of the tropics pressing down, the loneliness of cold grey wastes adrift with ice floes, the province of whale and tern. These, the factors of its setting, impart to the continent a specific and unique remoteness that has profoundly affected its destiny.

Into this land – whose nearest continental neighbours harbour man's earliest beginnings, oldest histories and more than half of the earth's people – a numerically small cluster of white people has been set down by the chances of history. As a people, the Australians are a good deal younger than the Age of Reason and any number of extant British tailors; even the sandwich has a continuous recorded history older than Australia's by 38 years.

But if the Australians are a comparatively recent and quirkful experiment in human history, their setting is not. At one time geology began its tables with what was called the Cambrian Period, this being the oldest time when there was reasonable evidence of the existence of life on the planet. Anything before this was classified as Pre-Cambrian, a loose reference for a time vaster than all subsequent geological time. Indeed, each of the two major eras comprising Pre-Cambrian time occupies a span of time longer than the 600 million years between us and the beginning of the Cambrian Period.

Roughly three-quarters of the surface of the Australian continent is comprised of outcrops of Pre-Cambrian rock, most of them worn down by wind, dust, frost, rain and time into a vast, low-lying plateau. Some scientists believe this is the largest and most intact great fragment of the ancient primal continent of Gondwanaland, which once linked what are now India, Africa, South America, Australia and Antarctica. This residue of the lost time from the earth's birth labours has been reasonably stable for about 500 million years. Parts of it – the 280,000 square miles of the barren wasteland in Western Australia which geologists have named Yilgarn, the eroded domes which form the Musgrave Ranges, and the bizarre monoliths of Ayers Rock and the Olgas in the Northern Territory – go back perhaps 1,000 or 2,000 million years. It is enough to say that few parts of the earth's surface are known to be older than this.

While parts of the world were still shifting, writhing and changing, throwing up Himalayas and Alps and Atlases and Cordilleras, Australia's extensive Pre-Cambrian area had already settled into its future shape. The continent had been formed and it was empty and already it was beginning to wear away under the rain, the wind and the dust. When man did finally come to this continent, on the most belated of his journeyings across the planet, he was faced by an awesome intimidation. He stepped from a crowded "Old" World into a "New" World, into an austere emptiness and a primeval silence. The shock of this confrontation has to this day left its mark upon him. Even now there are lonely immensities of Australia where one is overwhelmed by an essence of the primal and a silence so heavy that it is more than silence. It is as real as the sky colours, pewtered by heat or blue enamelled in the dawns or tomato-red at dusty sundowns. It is as real as time-smoothed contours of grotesque humped rocks laid bare as the bones of the greatest flat land mass on the face of the earth.

It is not surprising that Australia's poets and painters, whether aboriginal or of civilised experience, have peopled such a land with the figures of myth – titans and shapes in the sky and voices on the wind. Out in that eternal quiet there has never yet really been a place for people. An earlier lodger, the aborigine, has a legend which expresses that. When time was young, the legend says, the sky pressed upon the earth, and men and animals crawled on their bellies. One black man, yearning to stand up, contrived to insert a stick more or less vertically between earth and sky, and pushed, and so was able to stand and walk. But the weight of the sky half-bent the stick, which explains the origin of the boomerang. More recent arrivals hear it in the bush, where the land's voice is silence and the trees are still, their leaves slack, and finally, there is no decent tree for hundreds after hundreds of miles.

This way is the brooding heart of the land. Yet there is much beside it to give variation to the pattern. There are alpine stretches with winter snowfields more extensive than Switzerland's and dense, sometimes untrodden forests of trees among the mightiest in the world. There are Continental vineyards and tropical jungles, bucolic landscapes that seem clipped from England, rolling prairies and green geometries of agriculture, great reefs and atolls of coral, bleached deserts and lunar landscapes, coloured splendours of bird and tree and flower, a grandeur of coastal cliffs, an unrivalled magnificence of ocean beaches.

But behind these is always the brooding presence of the brown land. It is at the heart of all other things – on the palette of the aborigine, terracotta and umbers and ochre, touches of black and clay-white, of khaki and olive-drab; and in the red west wind that blows on Sydney, hot and drying, bearing a dust that mocks the complacency of middle-class housewives. In the Centre the well-bred greens of the cow pastures are forgotten, the patterned tidiness of clover and lucerne on the soft hill fades; now days end in opal colours and the red sky turns into a bruised mystery before it has made a sunset. One is left, at the end, with the predominance of the earth colours and the reminder of the ancient bones everywhere pushing through the skin, the rock or the red soil of the basalt, the granite, ironstone, sandstone. Generations of Australians nurtured at school on recitations of Dorothea Mackellar's poem, *My Country*, have intoned an earth-anthem to a "sunburnt country," a "wide brown land." This is what it is: the eternal presence of those ancient beginnings into which man has just begun to make his presumptuous intrusions.

He came about 10,000 years ago, recently enough in the history of emerging humanity, and he moved in from those outlying northern islands, walking over long-gone land bridges or drifting on logs or rafts to the random sweep of tidal currents, bringing with him his few primitive Stone Age things and that dog of his that was to become the dingo. He did not waken the sleeping land, but he multiplied and wandered and found his own myth in the great quietness, and for thousands of years he, too, was undisturbed. Yet his possession was tenuous, precarious in the huge sprawl of the place, and he was tolerated by the land only because he asked so little of it. There were almost three million empty square miles, but he clung to the safer areas and fringes, following the timid passive beasts of the land. His numbers never rose above a few hundred thousand, and time divided these into perhaps six hundred or more small and wandering tribes, widely scattered and speaking many different tongues, all of them melodious. He invented no wall or wheel, built no dwellings, planted no crops, learnt no writing, fathered no civilisation. He had little sense of future and he made no effort to find wealth or to develop sustenance from the soil under his calloused nomadic feet. What he did develop was the richest of primitive arts and mythology of his own – a complicated "Black Genesis," a "dreaming time" and pattern of life, a strange and rigid pastiche of giants and spirits, of totem and fetish, that only now is capturing the more sophisticated imaginations of our contemporary scholars and poets. The aborigine, then, had hardly touched the enormous land, and been hardly touched himself by time or change when the white man came to settle in the year 1788.

His was a very belated arrival on the scene, when you consider that a great mysterious "South Land" (and that is what the name Australia means) was guessed at, largely on the basis of a Chaldean tradition emanating from South India, by Roman scholars in the second century of the Christian era. *Terra Australis* or *Terra Incognita* teased the minds of geographers through the centuries that followed. Yet in the swiftly developing period of world exploration which followed Magellan's first circumnavigation of the globe, Australia was overlooked not because nobody *saw* it, but simply because nobody *wanted* it. It was, after all, too huge a lump of a thing not to be noticed. Here was an unbroken slab of land covering 2,944,866 square miles plus a satellite island of over 26,000 square miles. From tropical south latitudes it stretched all the way down to the cold wild seas of the Roaring Forties. From longitudes in the Indian Ocean it sprawled across more than 40 degrees of longitude to the Pacific. To circumnavigate its remarkably compact coastline would involve a voyage of 12,210 miles, roughly the distance from Sydney to London by way of the Suez Canal. As European kingdoms scoured the world for empires, here was the world's largest available block of real estate, empty.

But when the white man came at last to *Terra Incognita* – and this held true whether he was Portuguese, Spanish, Dutch, or English – he was led erroneously to believe that the country was absolutely worthless. He found a pitilessly unco-operative *Ultima Thule* lacking spices, rare metals, ancient treasure, worthwhile slaves, or even a patch of arable soil. A few naked savages, "the miserablest people in the world," as one of their first guests called them, scratched in the baking earth for reptiles and insects.

Even William Dampier, that unpiratically gentle buccaneer who preferred learned studies to making captives walk the plank or sacking Spanish cities, was disenchanted with his first look in 1688. His landfall on the inhospitable western shore was a low, bleak coastline of bone-bleached dunes and beyond, a drab brown stony desert, scrofulous with sickly vegetation. Of the natives he found there, he wryly noted: "The Hodmadods of Monomatpa, though a nasty people, are gentlemen to these." No prophetic vision told him of the immense mineral wealth that lay just beneath the skin of that unlovely landscape; he possessed no crystal ball in which he might have seen, on that grim rejecting coast, today's intricate complex of gigantic metal towers, taller than the Eiffel, where American technologists are building new monuments to the scientific audacities of twentieth century man.

It was by pure chance that all the first-comers, following the routes to the spice islands, found the cruellest, or most depressing corners of the land. They turned away, to a man, in unmitigated repugnance, and the space on the face of the globe sketchily limned as the Great South Land soon dropped into the discard of promise or afforded field for satire.

Forty-four years before Captain James Cook, in the name of England, took possession of eastern Australia (which at least looked rather more desirable than the *western* parts), Jonathan Swift wrote *Gulliver's Travels*. His mythical land of Lilliput, on the 30th parallel of south latitude, sat north-west of Van Diemen's land, smack in the middle of Australia. This location pivots now on the tiny railway township of Farina, near dry Lake Torrens which once turned explorer Charles Sturt back from the interior. It is not far, now, from the missile site of Woomera, which is named for the primitive spear-throwing stick of the Stone Age aboriginal people who nomadically still appear in these haunts. Jonathan Swift might have been vastly entertained by the paradoxical truth of his Lilliput – the complicated metal towers and gantries of the Nuclear-Space Age, cemented into the crustal rock of geology's Archaeozoic Era in a desert countryside where a Stone Age people still survives.

When eventually Australia did come to be peopled by other than the aborigines it was done with no flair of adventure, no feeling of enthusiasm, a marked lack of purposeful incentive, and a thoroughly grudging parsimony. Nothing about it even resembled the bold drive of human aspiration. Australia, in fact, was settled in the manner of somebody hiding something unpleasant away in an unwanted cupboard, hoping nobody would come across it.

With troubles at home and the loss of the American colonies, England needed outlets for the grim congestion of its brimming gaols – a new penal colony as far from the British Isles as possible, where problems would become too remote to be pressing and from which escape would be well nigh impossible. If such a colony forestalled the French and could also grow flax, from which to make canvas for the sails of ships of the King's Navy, so much the better. Thus did Australia become the chosen land.

At least the eastern seaboard which Cook had found and annexed looked comparatively fertile. Botanists had reported that the cultivation of flax was a possibility, the natives seemed neither hostile nor numerous, and there were no beasts of prey. There was ample timber, of a sort, for building, and the shores of the place chosen for settlement abounded in shellfish from which lime could be obtained. Above all, divine providence had fixed the place so far away, so hidden it under the curve of the earth, that once settled it would hardly need to be considered at all. At the outset, the British Government made it clear that it had no intention of squandering an unnecessary penny on a convict settlement on the other side of the world, a settlement to be hardly more populous, after all, than Newgate or the Fleet Prison or even Bedlam. Mounting difficulties in the war with France pushed forgetfulness to the brink of amnesia.

So under the first governor-designate, Captain Arthur Phillip, R.N., the frugally victualled, ill-found, and parsimoniously outfitted "First Fleet" of eleven small ships had filled up from the notorious prison hulks and sailed from the tight green shores of England on 13 May 1787 with 1,473 men and women, 778 of them convicts, including 192 female malcontents. In spite of romantic whitewashings since, almost all the prisoners were genuine criminals. There was a somewhat recalcitrant and sullen military guard of 200 marines and officers. In this forced and rather sordid exodus of Australia's founding fathers there was hardly a soul who had the least desire to go where he or she was being sent. The uncomfortable passage out lasted a week over eight months the first ships of the fleet reaching Botany Bay (almost precisely where the overseas jet airliners now land 30 hours out from England) on 18 and 19 January 1788. Finding Botany Bay insalubrious, they moved on a week later to the superb harbour of Port Jackson and, in a little shingly cove by a scraggy creek, raised the Union Jack and turned the first sods for what has since become the city of Sydney. This date, 26 January, is rather half-heartedly observed now as "Australia Day."

It was hardly a propitious beginning to a new land. The newcomers, free and chained alike, had been given practically nothing with which to deal with the scrubby, alien, forbidding, and remarkably strange surroundings in which they now found themselves. They saw the place as "unkempt, uncanny, and unknown."

The trees were different, the birds were different, the insects were different, colour was different, the light was different, the very scale of the landscape was different, sounds were different. The flowers, though violently chromatic and prodigal in variety, were without scent and strangely bristly. There was a profusion of insects of the oddest types and an extraordinary range of reptiles that seemed to have survived from some long lost world. The birds were bewildering, the fish improbable, the animals absurd. The aborigines seemed hardly to belong to a human species. The iron-hard eucalyptus trees defied axe and adze and auger. The soil had no affinity for the plough; indeed it must have laughed to feel the puny tickle of those first picks and shovels. And every dawn greeted the settlers with the crazed cackle of the kookaburra as if the land was mocking its reluctant invaders. It was as though the old continent could have thrown them all off with one brief shrug of its huge shoulders.

Governor Phillip, a fine man and considering everything a most uncomplaining one, reported with superb British understatement that no country had ever offered less assistance to its first settlers.

Since there was little hope of return to the safe familiarities of England, however, and at this stage no place to which to retreat, the first Australians had no alternative but to try to make the best of it. On a precarious little beachhead at the edge of an immense unknown continent they began to dig in. As a consolation for "home" one of the first recreational events of the embryo colony was a theatrical performance by the convicts of Farquhar's satirical play, *The Recruiting Officer*, staged almost exactly on the spot where the Australians of today are building a $50,000,000 Opera House which will be one of the architectural wonders of the world. Nor did the arrival of a "Second Fleet" bring relief. It brought only more convicts – "a ghastly company of sick and dying" who were the pitiable survivors of a long and dreadful passage that belongs in a world of nightmare. Of the provisions, stores, materials and tools so desperately needed, almost nothing arrived.

Until a few years ago it was the custom for Australians to draw a discreet curtain across these raw and hard beginnings. They preferred to see their convict forefathers either as the more or less innocent victims of social injustice or political oppression, or to over-glorify the early free settlers and true "pioneers" at the expense of the felonry. A wiser, more mature outlook has since come to understand that some of the strongest threads in the Australian character run all the way back to those days when the country, in effect, was not much more than a huge, sprawling, uniquely underprivileged British gaol. For many of the roots of Australian strength and identity – the toughness and tenacity, the resourcefulness and initiative, the firm rejection of class and caste, the mordant humour, even elements of the national mythology – derive from those wretched beginnings.

It is true that even up to the time of the gold rushes of the early 1850s – when the land nobody had wanted gave the first sensational indication of its enormous riches — Australia was remarkable in the eyes of all overseas visitors for the drunkenness and profanity of its people, the looseness of its women (at that time far outnumbered by men), the crudity of its social manners, the shakiness of its ethics and moralities, and the sturdy independence of its people. It is also true that by this time, of approximately 60,000 convicts transported to the New South Wales Colony, more than 38,000 had survived chains, lash, tyranny and exploitation to rise to free, respectable and creditable positions in colonial life.

In the early phases a privileged or astute few had grabbed the richest of the land, and the comparatively fertile seaboard tracts grudgingly succumbed to a still-precarious pattern of settlement. But attempts to impose a colonial version of English-style aristocracy of landed gentry was fiercely opposed, short-lived and, finally, futile. Instead, there emerged a rough-and-ready, never specified code of colonial ethics. Conceived under convict conditions it had by the 1850s solidified into a kind of general behaviour pattern for all but the few self-styled aristocrats and a clutch of military and government officials. It was common to convict, emancipist, "Currency" lad, and in fact to all but the new immigrant, who still had to prove he could cope with his unique and chastening environment.

From the early and intensely masculine conditioning imposed during stubborn attempts to settle and subdue even a beachhead on this monstrous continent, there evolved a strong sense of social solidarity and general mistrust of imposed authority. With this came a detestation of the "pimp" or informer, of the "crawler," the "skite" or boaster, of the man who "whinged" or complained of his lot. Prospectors, shearers, drovers, bullockies, fettlers or farmhands, each was entitled to his "fair go," and until proven otherwise any man was as good as the next one. It was perhaps a crude code of ethics, but no other country ever succeeded in creating a virtually classless society in so brief a time from such very dubious beginnings. Within two or three generations a distinct and separate people were developing out of what had begun as almost one hundred per cent British stock. They were already different in speech, physique, attitudes, social consciousness, manners, and even to some degree in physiognomy. They were a new people, these Australians. Then, as now, theirs was a country where there was more work than Australians to do it, and an uncompromising environment in which to battle. But whether bond or free, very few settlers ever went back to Europe, even after there was nothing to prevent them.

In the beginning, of course, their beachhead was more of a toehold, hardly more than tentative scratchings at the giant. Yet however briskly the new arrivals debated the virtues of Protestantism, the rights of emancipists and the treatment of the bewildered aboriginals, they could not long ignore the inland vastness. There were different drives to spur them as individuals – land hunger, the primitive urge to find pastoral sustenance for themselves and their families. Some went on believing in dreams, as men do, of Big Rock Candy Mountains; some for the stubborn hell of it, as Mallory would go to Everest. Later they would go in a feverish quest for precious metals, convinced the country was suddenly an El Dorado, though only a handful would win fortunes. But in the beginning the greatest urge was for new land for their sheep, the new arrivals the old land seemed to tolerate most easily.

The slumbering giant yielded its ground only grudgingly. Not until 1813, a quarter of a century after Botany Bay, did Governor Lachlan Macquarie's men find a way over the Blue Mountains, 66 miles from Sydney. Explorers who followed, such as the intrepid John Oxley, turned back again and again in despair at the harsh and arid land, or the fact that the Lachlan River seemed to end alternately in trackless marshes or dry beds, depending on the climate that year. Repeatedly, the early searches for a great inland sea yielded only hardscrabble sand; green river valleys like those of the Hastings were infrequent consolations. Not until 1824 did William Hilton Hovell and Hamilton Hume walk their way to Port Phillip, finding the luxuriant valley of the Murray and the surrounding pastoral lands which would one day fatten the merino into the finest wool-bearing animal in the world. Three years later the botanist Allan Cunningham edged north and found the grazing lands of Darling Downs, and before the decade was out the way was opened to Victoria and South Australia.

Yet these were the merest tentative probings, never too far from the sea and timid in relation to the size of the adversary. Even Eyre, the first to cross to the western coast, stayed so close to the ocean that his greatest aid came from the nautical charts of the navigator Matthew Flinders. For whatever their objective or spur, and whichever their routes of attack, the early explorers and the few hardy settlers who tried to follow them always ended confronted by the trackless, virtually waterless, and wholly intimidating wilderness a million square miles in extent, a thousand miles one way and a thousand miles the other, all of it unexplored and much of it obviously unexplorable. They were either forced back to the safer coastal settlements from which they had set out, or obliged to make the best of a bad thing and "have a go" at the exceedingly hard yet barely possible country surrounding the "Dead Heart."

By far the greatest area of the land that was of any use at all seemed useful only for cattle, and even at that was often so poor that properties covering thousands of square miles would be needed to carry herds economically. Victoria River Downs cattle station, until subdivided a few years ago, covered nearly 12,000 square miles — a single ranch as big as Belgium, half as big again as all Israel. The Costello-Durack holding centred on Cooper Creek covered 17,000 square miles, or 10,880,000 acres at the time the families moved off on their great overland trek to pioneer the Kimberleys.

In the opening up of the North American continent the frontiersman had had difficulties to combat, but he found soft prairies somewhere across his mountains and herds of game, and lush fields and fair forests and flowing rivers on the other sides of his deserts. There *were* rewards beyond almost every new horizon. America had desperate areas and proud hostile natives, but it was not a geological nightmare, and it was said that in the frontier days a squirrel could have crossed North America from Atlantic to Pacific without ever having to come down out of the trees.

It was a very different story in Australia, and it is not surprising that there were no Lewises or Clarks. The Australian pioneer found every frontier dribbling away into the shimmer of mirage, into wastes of sand or dry gibber or hard-caked saltpans or weirdly eroded mountain ranges of Pre-Cambrian rocks. He could be brought up short by any one of Australia's four vast deserts, each containing areas bigger than European countries, and which to this day have rarely been trodden by man. If his journeys were made in the hot seasons, temperatures could range from the merely cruel to the lethal. As man later logged the figures, heat of 127.5 Fahrenheit in the shade was recorded officially at Cloncurry, in Queensland, and of 133 unofficially in Central Australia.

Marble Bar, in Western Australia, holds the town record for sustained heat; from October 1923, until April 1924, the shade temperature never dropped below 100 for 160 consecutive days. But the pioneer's journeys were often in places where there was no shade, for in some of these blistering wastelands no plant life grows even waist-high, and here he could broil in sun temperatures exceeding 155. He found little or no game. Water became his and a national obsession.

Here again everything was crazy, topsy-turvy, paradoxical. In a given area he could be almost drowned in the hammering deluge of monsoonal rains, see great rivers in torrent running away to waste and yielding, because of intense evaporation, to a parched, cracked earth two weeks later. As easily, he could find dried-up watercourses gouged through bizarre landscapes desiccated by years of unbroken drought. Like the tentacles of an octopus the misleading courses of dry river-beds mark the map around misnamed Lake Eyre, in South Australia. Not really a lake at all but the lowest piece of the continent, Eyre like the Dead Sea is substantially below sea level; the rivers "running" into it are mere dry traces to guide the fruitless spillings of rare if violent cloudbursts. The Macumba, the Warburton, the Finke, Cooper Creek, the Neales – rivers? This is the driest area of the whole continent. There are parts where no drop of rain has fallen in years, and much of this area has not averaged even a five-inch annual rainfall this century. Sydney, by contrast, averages 47 inches a year, and Australia's wettest town, Tully in North Queensland, has recorded 311 inches. But for Australian pioneers there were no Mississippis, no Missouris, no Columbias. When Ernest Giles, the last of Australia's inland explorers, wrote that "exploration of one thousand miles in Australia is equal to ten thousand miles in any other part of the earth's surface," he excepted only the Arctic and the Antarctic.

There is an odd, almost dreamlike quality to the Australian explorer stories. They are always faintly Kafka-esque, dislodged from everyday reason. Eyre treks 1,500 miles west from Spencer Gulf to King George's Sound, and writes of 1,500 miles without once meeting running water. Mad Ludwig Leichhardt goes south into the desert, leading a party of six men, fifty bullocks, twenty mules and seven horses and all vanish, totally without trace. Eighty-four living things vanish in the desert and never a bone is found and the best solution offered for the mystery is that all were swallowed in a rare torrent from Cooper Creek. And it is true that Cooper Creek in flood can overflow its dry banks until it is 40 or 50 miles wide. Burke and Wills, half-dead of starvation, stagger back to their base camp to find the main party had given up on them and retreated towards the sea earlier that day, and so complete their dying. Impelled by conviction in a great inland sea, steady Captain Charles Sturt hurls himself again and again into the "heartless desert" and writes seriously in his journals of a member of his party glimpsing that non-existent sea, "deep blue and in it a conical island of great height."

"It does not read like history," wrote Mark Twain, a man with an eye always cocked for an oddity, "but like the most beautiful of lies; and all of a fresh new sort, no mouldy old stale ones." But there were no lies about the bushflies that bedevilled the explorers' eyes and mouths, turning their days into ordeals which matched the agonies of nights when ants crawled in biting armies over their exhausted bodies, or about their permanently injured eyes, bruised by the implacable sun. Fitting, then, that Sidney Nolan, the painter, and Patrick White the novelist are almost surrealistic in their separate approaches to the explorer stories. Birds are upside down in bizarre landscapes and men are mad.

Yet men did follow, slowly, the track of these explorers and the prospectors who later followed them. And for the follower, too, fresh from the isles of Britain, everything was upside down. The solstices were reversed. His midsummer night's dream was more of a nightmare, the coldest time of the year. On Christmas Day, when his memories were of yule logs and snowmen and ice on the ponds, the sun broiled like a furnace. Even the heavenly constellations were upside down or totally unfamiliar. In this land of the dry-living plants, the *xerophytes*, there seemed nothing soft and nothing green – only the bizarre and prickly banksia and mallee and spinifex and chittock, the grotesquerie of baobab and blackboy, or the endless repetition of grey-brown listless trees that shed their bark and kept their leaves, though the leaves all hung down as if exhausted.

In such a land, there were no clear-cut victories; the hero-figure never emerged as part of the national mythology as it did from the American Wild West. There are no gunfighters in Australian frontier legend; the last surviving fragment of Gondwanaland is chasteningly unresponsive to man's struttings and posturings and it inhibits the singer of sagas. Here man's rivals are rabbits and kangaroos, who bite the grass below the ground level, loosening the soil so that the next red wind will blow it away, and men learnt to write and sing of a land "where the crow flies backwards to keep the dust out of his eyes." Here men who moved inland, beyond the fences of the settled graziers and their fat-fleeced merino flocks, are called "the battlers."

They had their own apocalyptic four horsemen – drought, erosion, suffering or death by thirst or starvation, the annual devastation of bushfires, that periodic lashing back of the land against its invaders. When the battler did find rivers they sank into the sand and vanished quietly into deserts. His lakes were terrible, salt-rimed, brine-bitter and sometimes only fatal hallucinations of water. He drilled for water; it came up brown, brackish, boiling. He stumbled across melancholy plains stretching into infinities of loneliness, and insanely twisted landscapes, lunar rather than terrestrial. Most dispiriting and unnerving of all, he was almost everywhere made to feel that his was the first footfall to breach that aching silence; apart from stone axes and the occasional crude aboriginal tool there was never indication, in a crumbling wall, a shard of pottery, or the cold ashes of a fire, that any human creature had ever been this way before.

Nevertheless, whether explorer or squatter, selector or cattle man or nomadic battler, he fell in thrall to the land's perverse but compelling beauty. He struggled on obstinately, establishing his staging posts, making his marks, putting his roots down. Slowly he scratched his tenuous trails across this giant fragment of Gondwanaland until the roads and trails of his journeyings covered half a million miles and there were tens of thousands of his settlements scattered over the once-empty continent.

If it was too soon for him to win, if within him there remained, deep down in his bones, a tiny arthritic knuckle of uneasiness, as if he could not finally be absolutely sure of the security of his tenure, the Australian had still won his foothold. His was the flattest, the most barren, the most arid, the least fertile, the most sparsely populated, the most isolated of the continents, the one most unsympathetic, in other words, to man's aspirations. But in this land that sought to murder ambition with its massive indifference he had made a beginning. He had begun to shape, and be shaped by, the majesty of the challenge.

WE WERE FOLLOWING the stock up from Ivanhoe Crossing where there was not even a trickle of water, just hot sands and a few smelly lagoons trapped in a tumble of basalt boulders and the raucous screech of white cockatoos in the high pandanus.

Up North and in the West they have just been through some bad years. We had seen them in the Territory on their cattle runs, into their seventh year of drought, and every beast that still survived carried a debt of $20 on its head. Out in the Kimberleys some of the big stations had no cattle worth the mustering.

We caught up to the mob half-way to the meat works at Wyndham. They were a scraggy half-dead bunch, dusty hides draped on dead bones, listless around the bore tank. Only a few hundred had survived the drove. It didn't look like too many of them would make it the rest of the way, or be worth much even if they did.

Six skinny black stockmen in coloured shirts were tilted in their saddles like bent twigs and the smell of the drought was in the unmoving air. Beyond the windmill and the low line of scrub a series of shallow stony rises, the gibber glinting in the sun, rose to a clump of three ghost gums bone-white against a black rock-fall, then recessed into the enamelled sky behind the blood-red jump-ups and escarpments of the dry plateau.

The white stockman rolled himself a thin cigarette – a racehorse, he called it – and bit the end off and talked of cattle. Not of the dejected beasts around the bore tank, but of the big musterings, and the great droves. In his laconic way he was intensely possessive of

RIGHT) Dead ram, Witchelina Station, South Australia.

these vast dry empires in which he had his being. We talked of mineral development on the rangelands and plans for new pasture legumes and of irrigation and tropical crops and he nodded with careful consideration over these ambitioned plans and dreams of other men.

Above the slimed tank the windmill clanked lugubriously, and there was the lethargic *thuk* of the stockwhip in a stockman's black hand. "Yes, but this is cattle country," he said finally. "It always has been. Always will be. Just cattle country . . . ."

Out there it's always hard to give a scale to things. All space and no perspective, an absence of vanishing points, there's nothing to measure by . . . .

At Finke Gorge, in the Macdonnell Ranges, I once picked up a greenish brown stone, gorgeous in feel and colour. Some rare mineral, I thought, and cousin to a jewel, and for months I kept it in my pocket, fingering it. Finally a geologist identified it. A fragment of a broken beer bottle, worn and textured by occasional rain and wind-driven dust and grits.

I should have known what nature does there, creating patterns and

RIGHT) Wind-formed sand ridges from the air, Simpson Desert, western Queensland.

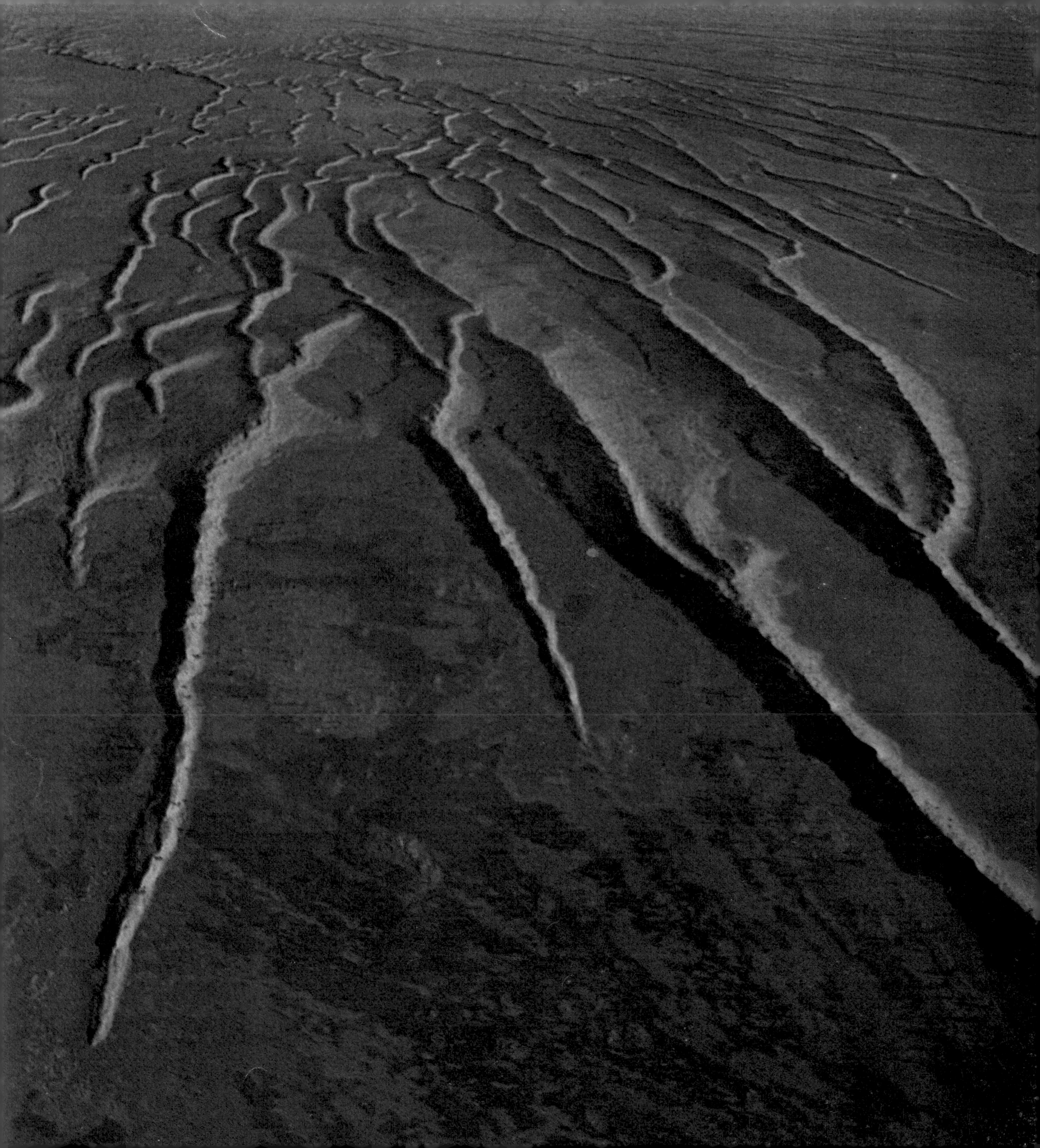

shapes, patina and texture, and appreciated the patience of its works. After the earth convulsions of the Ordovician Period the Macdonnells were mountains of pure rock, lacking life, bare even of the most primitive lichens, but soaring to summits of 10,000 to 15,000 feet. After that, there were no further great earth movements to twist and mould the geography of the Centre, only sun and rain, wind, frost, dust and grit. But during the next 500 million years this unrelenting erosion rubbed 12,000 feet of the proud peaks away,

LEFT) Sunrise on the Olgas, Northern Territory.
BELOW) Giant Red Kangaroo, near Farina, South Australia.

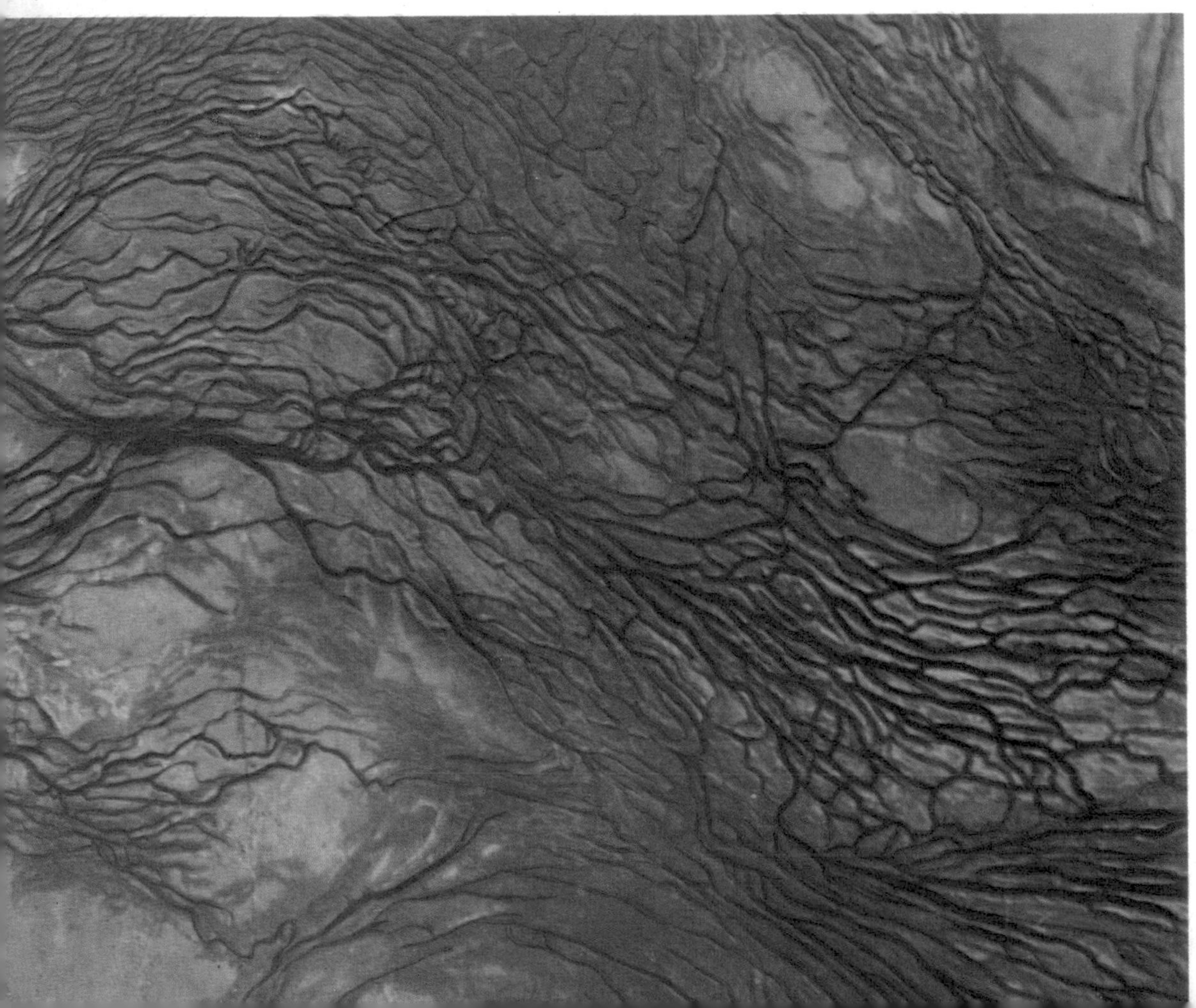

and gave this fabulous textured beauty to the landscape, dunes and rock-twists, the emu-feathered veinery of the channels, the capped and fissured monoliths.

So there is nothing marvellous about a scrap of broken beer bottle. Yet I still treasure it . . . .

In the beginning there was the land. The Biblical phraseology echoes in one's thoughts. In the space and empty quiet of the Centre all sense of human time is lost: it is both before time and outside it, as if

TOP LEFT) Sand dunes from the air, Finke River, Northern Territory.
TOP RIGHT) Sand dune detail, Finke River.
BOTTOM LEFT) Diamantina channel country, south-west Queensland.
BOTTOM RIGHT) Krichauff Range, south-west of Alice Springs, Northern Territory.
RIGHT) Ayers Rock detail, Northern Territory.

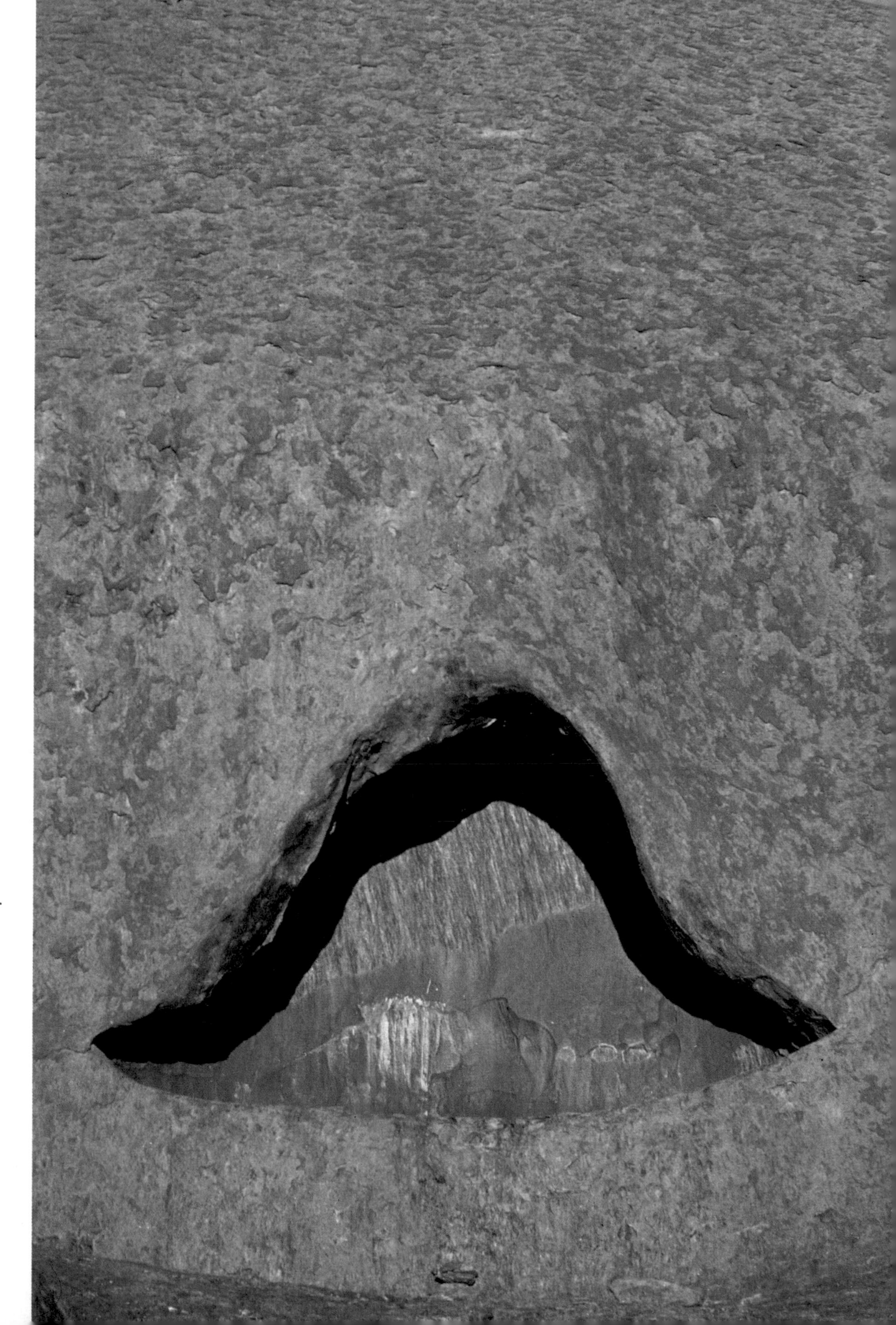

creation's moment is eternally recurring. Whatever happens seems to be happening beyond human experience, across a gap of undimensional, universal space. Perhaps this is what the aboriginal means by "the dreaming time . . . ."

Years may pass without a raindrop falling. A bushman said to a thirsting mate: "Don't go bankin' on *that* to fill the waterbags. People round these parts 'ave 'ad their eye on that cloud for the last five years . . . ."

We live in the debris of a fury. The Musgrave Ranges may be anything up to 2,000 million years old, the

LEFT) Rain squall, Northern Territory.

Snowy Mountains no older than one million; the one eroded down to nothing, hardly above sea level, the other thrown up from some other vast and featureless plain. This last is the Kosciusko Uplift, and it shaped the eastern land all the way from New Guinea to Tasmania, gave us harbours and rivers, the Blue Mountains and the Bass Strait, the snow country and solidified volcano cores, islands and lava flows and reefs, and the scattered debris of granite and basalt. We live where we can in the spoil and wreckage of this time of tumult . . .

Most of us have already turned away from the brown heart of the old land to this new crescent on its rim, where we can make our shelters less uneasily. And Outback people always talk, wistfully, of taking their holidays by the sea, even when the sea is a thousand miles away. I have always felt both are ritual to a more profound retreat . . . .

You come out of the North or the Heart to the eastern sea and there are jungled mountains, sweeping beaches,

LEFT) Snowy Mountains, New South Wales. Highest elevation: Mt. Kosciusko, 7,314 feet.
RIGHT) Basalt boulders, Black Mountains, North Queensland.

seas turquoise or emerald or indigo so deep that it can be almost black. And in these Pacific blues there stretches the Great Barrier Reef, the world's mightiest, most fascinating coral formation. It is the biggest thing on earth to be built by living creatures, and it is well to remember that this majestic work was built with no help at all from the hand of man; the polyps who made each of its 1,260 spectacular miles are often no bigger than a pin's head.

Yet the Reef, I think, is a place for happy people. The last time I was there I met a man in torn shorts who owned his own island; I met an amateur conchologist who was building up his shell museum, a leathery old fellow with a shack and a flat-bottomed boat who showed me the way of fishing for giant crabs in the mangroves, a half-caste trochus-fisher who showed me a dugong rolling in the shallows, and a man in the white sand beneath a coconut palm who was drying seahorses . . . .

Once the Burdekin River was in flood, and it rose 55 feet in one night and poured so much rainwater into the sea that coastal ships were pulling up buckets of fresh water eight miles offshore, and on the coral reefs all marine life was killed to a

LEFT) Seaward edge Great Barrier Reef, east of Lindeman Island, Queensland.
CENTRE, TOP TO BOTTOM) Giant Clam (*Tridacna*); Blue Sea-Star (*Linckia*); Abalone (*Teinotis*), Great Barrier Reef.
RIGHT) Tidal pools from the air, Great Barrier Reef, Queensland.

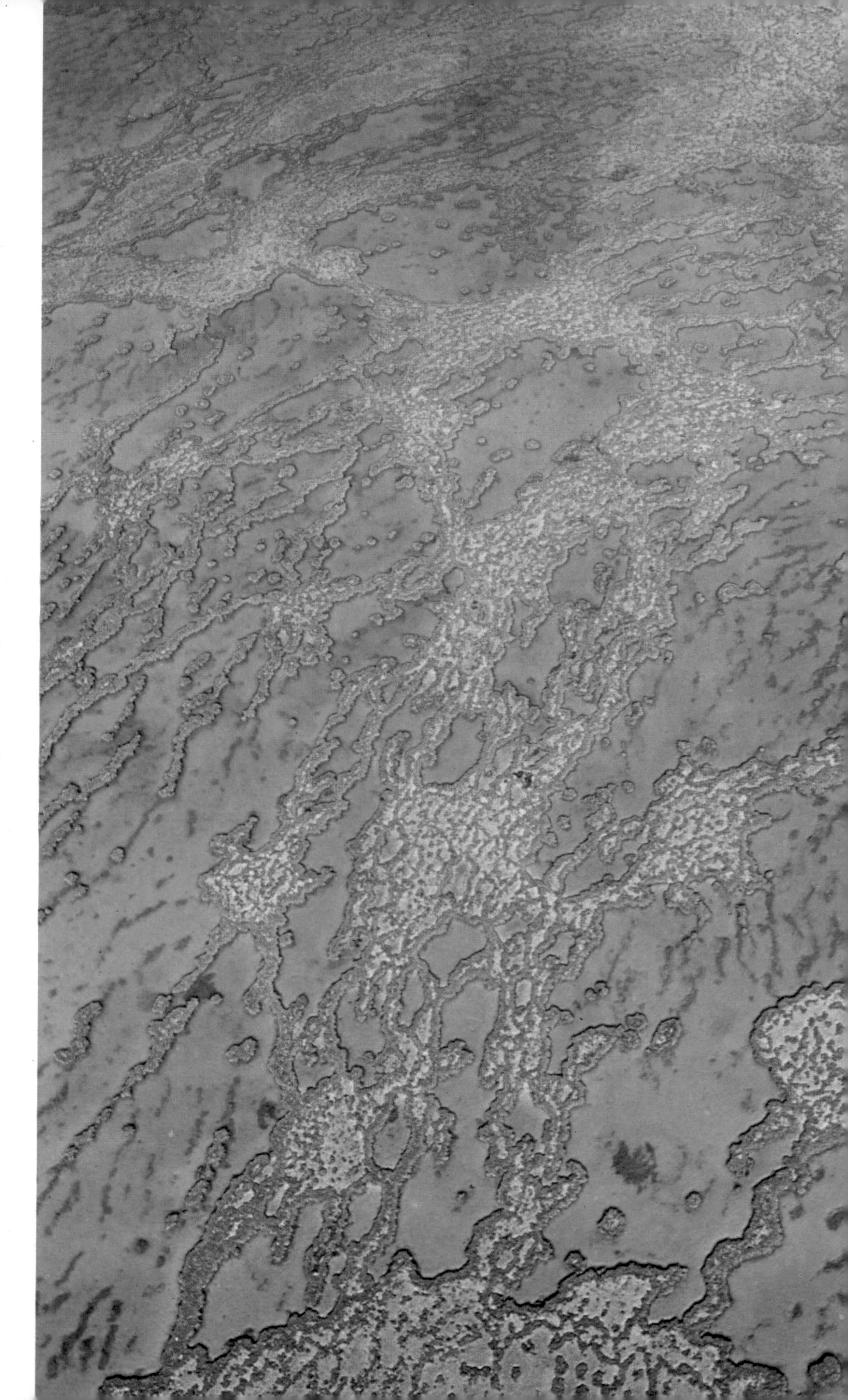

depth of ten feet. Inland, drought had struck and the cattle were dying for want of water.

For the biggest joke about Australia is rain. It either doesn't come at all or it comes in great indigestible gulps. So we find, on earth's most arid continent, dense tropical jungles, the rioting tangle of temperate rain forests, the python twist of river estuaries and deltas wasting into the sea. There is a place in North Queensland where 35.71 inches of rain – a fraction short of a yard of it – has fallen in a day, other places where that much doesn't fall in ten years.

I find in an old notebook two quotations scribbled. The first is from a scientist: "We shall triumph eventually over the treachery of our rain and the obstinacy of our rivers." The other from a publican in South Australia: "The reason why we're all big beer drinkers is we've got to save the water to keep the blasted geraniums alive . . . ."

Where rainfall comes in some rational pattern, where we have clustered thickest on the edge,

LEFT) Rain forest, Ferntree Gully, Victoria.
RIGHT) Mouth of the Fitzroy River, Queensland.

the land can smile. Then there comes a smell that is very Australian, that thin subtle odour of "the bush," an unmistakable pungency of grass and tussocks and bark and the faintest suggestion of aromatic oils stealing out from the trees. I remember the shock of recognition, coming back to it after an absence abroad of many years. I had been nostalgic for other Australians, and had forgotten this. The green pastures and the slow drift of flocks, lambs on the twist of legs weak and tentative, the broom out on the hill. There is much that is tranquil and good where man has made his settlements, even if

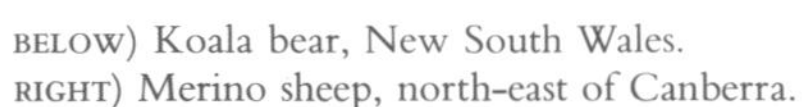

BELOW) Koala bear, New South Wales.
RIGHT) Merino sheep, north-east of Canberra.

FIRE

hawk and crow and eagle are still aloft and vigilant . . . .

D. H. Lawrence, in Sydney but still haunted by the bush, once wrote of an aborigine boy "lost so many centuries on the margin of existence." I think the land dictates this marginal occupancy; and the earlier black lodger came to terms with it. He followed the game and the rains and the run of the streams, not trying to tame the land, but living in it and with it. In his rich mythology, earth and sky, rain and drought, survival and death and fire and ashes, rock cave and billabong, and all living creatures and inanimate things were united in a single harmony, all parts of himself. And in this simple state the land allowed him.

Our tread is heavier; we move to stronger ambitions. We try to press beyond the margins, and the land strikes back . . . .

LEFT) Volunteer bushfire brigade, south of Sydney, New South Wales.
RIGHT) Pitjantjatjara aborigine, Ernabella Mission Station, South Australia.

When I was a schoolboy my Uncle Wattie used to tell us stories of the great drought, eight years long, that broke in 1903. It killed, he said, half of all the animals grazed and pastured in Australia. Wattie was only a courtesy uncle, a "Geordie" from Tyneside with grey flannel bands sewn round rheumaticky fingers which were always tamping stubby broken pipes. He had a scrubby, quartzy little selection farm in old diggings country near Corindhap in Victoria.

We never really believed these stark dramatic tales because he always told them in good or idle times, when we were fishing for eels or perch in the Battery Dam below Chinner's woolshed, when the wheat was high and green and the clay paddock-dam yellow-full and lively with yabbies and his own meagre wool clip was selling at 20 pence a pound at the Ballarat or Geelong sales. This was all years ago, and these were an old man's cautionary tales told in fat seasons as touchstone against the lean.

We listened wide-eyed, not realising that it had all been true until years afterwards, when Old Wattie's selection was no more than a fire-charred memento overgrown with bracken. He was dead, his sons gone from the place, and the rabbits back in their sandy squats.

LEFT) Hotel veranda, south-west Queensland.

The Land's People

Once there was a doughty people in the land, but all save the very old among them are dead now. The wind blows dust and leaves and scraps of dead bark across simple graves in Snake Gully and Black Jack's Creek and Ironbark Flats, and the impedimenta of a whole lost age rusts away in a paddock or collapsed slab humpy or derelict woolshed. The folk-verse and balladry of their time are city-sung now, guitar-strummed by a new generation of bearded young men in blue jeans and girls with long smooth hair.

The earlier ones were in many ways a limited people, close to the earth, brave and stubborn, laconic. Their lives were simple, harshly delineated by blue hills, the sullen glow of fire in the ranges, the stand of stringybark above the old battery dam. Their times were measured by the pace of the rams and ewes moving, kelpie-driven, to the dip, by the slow jog of the Afghan peddler's waggon and the clip-clop of a whickering old bay mare between the buggy-shafts, driving to Sunday meetings at the tiny weatherboard church in a paddock where the ring-barked ghost trees stood more pallid than the tombstones.

These were the small selection farmers who went and built the Australian country out of a huge and shapeless world, the "bush people" who lived behind post-and-rail fences daubed with the advertised familiarities of their generations—*112 Miles to Griffiths Tea, Reckitt's Blue for a Whiter Wash, Try Goanna Salve*—and they fixed the rural patterns for the better part of a century.

It was a slow, painstaking time of individualism and muscle and a lifetime's sweat. But slowly it opened wheat lands and cattle lands and sheep lands and timber camps and the shafts of mines, and it spread the Australian people into the big land across roads and tracks and stock routes. They built the farms and made the homesteads and the townships and the saleyards and the country pubs and the wheat sidings, and pretty much all of this was a hand-hewn world that man created.

If material truth and symbolic poetry were to define a national memorial, then Australia's monument might fittingly be the preservation of just one of the old selectioner's slab cottages with its roof and chimney of corrugated iron, and ringed water tank, and walls and outhouses textured with a pasted collage of old newspapers and country magazines.

This traditional Australian picture is still much-preserved abroad, and sentimentally clung to even by a good many contemporary Australians. The picture is a crystallisation of this long period; it was a time which formed and still pervades much of popular art and literature, which consolidated social patterns and mythologies, and which stirred the present deep interest by Australians in their own "Australiana." It was the time of gold rushes and the Eureka Stockade, of bushrangers and Ned Kelly, of Henry Lawson and the social solidarities of "mateship," of Banjo Paterson and *Waltzing Matilda*, of the wry and rollicking and "typically Australian" humour of Dad and Dave and Steele Rudd's *On Our Selection*. It was the time both of *The Anzac Book* and *The Sentimental Bloke*. It was, in fact, the crucible of the Australian image.

It began with the first of the great gold rushes, this time of the most courageous penetration of the empty land, and many of the harshest and some of the richest areas of the continent were to be opened initially by gold prospectors. When the rushes began in 1851, less than half a million acres of Australian land were under cultivation, and even this small area diminished as men rushed off to the diggings. Yet by the end of that decade the coming of new settlers had doubled the rural holdings to over a million acres. And as the holdings and habitations of man spread slowly and more widely through the enormous land, they followed the trails blazed by prospector or individual adventurer more often than those marked by the explorer. Always there was a very thin scattering of humanity through a very great extent of physical space. It continued in spite of seven catastrophic droughts, one of which lasted eight years and killed half the sheep and nearly half the cattle in Australia, and many smaller localised "crook seasons." It survived speculative land booms and their disastrous sequels in the last century. It endured the effects of this century's wars and economic setbacks, and the natural depredations of pest, flood and fire, and man's own manifold errors of judgement. At the turn of the century a stake in the great continent had been achieved for fewer than four million people, for fewer than six million even after the end of World War I, for only seven million by the beginning of World War II.

In the face of man's small victories the land itself continued to impose the limitations that dictated the human pattern, and built a mould of people as well as a way of life. To this day the working resident of the inland areas, whether grazier or stockman, prosperous farmer or fringe battler, is almost always recognisable among a ruck of city men by the shape of a hat, something of stance, a particular quality in the eyes, a way of pausing between sentences as if there is time to make sure of what one is saying. The common denominator of their bearings springs from a mutually shared experience.

Drought, cattle tick, bad seasons, frosts, vermin, bushfires, glutted markets, tariff barriers, slumps, these strike the wealthy grazier as impartially as the small battler. There are wealthy graziers who live social calendar lives on what are near enough to princely estates, with polo games and junketings to Europe and private air-strips and stud stock in the paddocks and blue ribbons in the harness rooms. Their sons are at the best schools and their daughters curtsey at the Queen Charlotte's Ball in London. But they have always been judged finally and irrevocably on the quality of their wool, the condition of their stock, the yield of their crops, and the manner in which their hands are treated. In the material sense Jack may not be as good as his master, but Jack shares the run of the seasons, dependent upon the earth. When Australian armies volunteered for war, as they always used to do, the propertied grazier or his station manager was frequently the private in the ranks, often with the station rouseabout or boundary-rider as the commissioned officer.

There are rich properties in Australia and splendid homesteads, but there are no "stately homes" or enclaves of privilege in yeoman country, no close preserves for "rough shooting" jealously guarded by lynx-eyed gamekeepers, no landed gentry in the older usage of the phrase. Everything is far too big and spread out, exposed to the sun and wind and sky. The dust whirls across dry paddocks without regard to fences, the flies will blow the big grazier's prize merino as foully as the smaller farmer's crossbred, the crows and eagles answer to no protocol when a ewe is down or a lamb ailing.

So it was less from social circumstance that the principles of "mateship" sprang, than from those "brute facts of Australian geography." Mateship, that peculiarly Australian sub-philosophy, was a product of the immense distances and utter loneliness of "the bush," of the stupefying scale of space and emptiness and raw nature in which man had to contend for survival. From these brute facts came the strong sense of social solidarity, the ingrained sense of the rights of individuals with its rigid rule that every man was entitled to a "fair go." For in such a country the enormity was too much not to be shared.

Here now a single property can cover thousands of square miles, a nearest neighbour may live 200 miles away, the front gate of a property can be 30 miles from the front door. Here nothing is thought of hopping into a car and driving a couple of hundred miles each way for a dance or a social evening or just to follow the district cricket or football team. Here the daily milk delivery at Mount Isa comes 700 miles from the Atherton Tableland. And the members of Mount Isa's amateur dramatic company have travelled 1,000 miles by road to Alice Springs to perform a one-act play, only to find they have mistaken the date, and so drive all the way back again, and cheerfully repeat the trip a week later.

Here man has now been able to add the ingenuity of his machines to the stubbornness of his spirit to achieve mastery over the basic inland problem – the vastness of space and the distance between people. Today's Australians of the Outback have used the new marvels of radio and aviation to whittle further at the barriers of isolation and loneliness, to bring education to the scattered children of the Outback, medical aid to the sick or injured, social communion to men and women committed in places of solitude where once the outside world was the arrival at six-monthly intervals of a lumbering bullock-train.

Radio means the "Galah Session" every morning when housewives can swap gossip over tens of thousands of square miles. Formal rhythms are now keyed to the comings and goings of the little planes of the bush pilots' services or the airliners covering the intricate networks of the station runs, to the Flying Doctor Service and the Radio School of the Air. The outback dweller now talks with an unbelieving little shake of the head of what it was like in the days before radio and airplane.

In the land where fossickers pushed wheelbarrows or rode bicycles thousands of miles to get from old diggings to new ones, the leathery few oldtimers with their swag rolls and canvas waterbags and blackened quart billies and hand tools and washpans and flour for damper have taken their secret journeys now to distant corners, to the north-west and the other frontiers of Western Australia. They log their nomadic travel in decades now and not in miles.

The legendary swagman is now a stranger in the country towns of Australia, where Main Street on a Saturday morning, when the farmers and their wives come in, has a quality of formality as precise and beautiful as a minuet. It is true that there remains a rhythm to life in the towns that cities are losing or have lost – a deeper dependence on human interrelationships than on synthesised entertainments, a sense of things moving within orbits of experience that are understood and shared. But the skimpy grasp on the land of a century ago, with a few coastal settlers on less than half a million acres, has grown to over a quarter of a million separate rural holdings covering 1,178 million acres. And most of the country towns' pasts are in their names, so many of them drawn from that melodious litany that is the legacy from the aborigine. Minnamurra, Ulladulla, Koonoongoonang, Toolangi.

Whatever the tune of its name there will be an old pub on the corner called the Station or the Grand or the Royal or the Imperial, with painted beer signs and pillared verandas and gracious balcony railings of cast-iron that came a century ago as ballast for the wool clippers. Now there is a prosperity of parked cars along both sides of the wide main street. The clock under the tin gables of the rickety old Mechanics' Institute is obstinate at twenty-to-eleven; the townspeople can no more remember when the hands moved last than recall who the mechanics were. The Country Women's Association is getting ready for a bazaar for crippled children; in a marquee alongside the church hall women move amid a wealth of home-made cakes and crochet, bottled preserves and knitted layettes, and jellies luminous as stained glass in mediaeval churches. At a table adorned with paper flowers two committee women number the books of tickets for the raffle of Steve Cassidy's ducklings.

In the street across from the hotel, six men with shirtsleeves rolled high on mahogany arms sit on the steps of the war memorial appraising silently the new 12-disc plough, gay in bright orange paint. Five of the six men have names the same as some chiselled into the plinth of the Anzac memorial, which features the white marble figure of a man in a slouch hat and puttees leaning on a reversed rifle. Below this curiously squat effigy there is a double column of names under the inscription "For King and Country . . . 1914-1918." On the reverse face of the memorial, where a faded wreath lies, is more sharply chiselled the legend "Lest We Forget . . . 1939-1945" above three columns of names. The town grew between the wars, but the names of this side duplicate the ones of the other. Once a year, on Anzac Day, the memorial is hardly to be seen for flowers and wreaths; otherwise it is a place to sit and look at things.

But the peopling of the land in Australia has never been a static thing, and this town is luckier than some: some never recovered from the single fact that whole surrounding districts were denuded of their able-bodied young men, volunteers for war in 1914 and 1915, and only a handful ever returned; others fell as the tides of change washed against their districts and shifted the purposes of people. In the north-west the cyclones blow a town away, a pearling port decays, life ebbs from a gold town or a hamlet in the gem fields, the beef roads and the big cattle road trains leave in twilight a town on the old stock route built amid the anthills with a main street a hundred yards wide for the mobs mustering through. The cities lure the young away from the old wool port on the river where paddle steamers no longer ply, from the sleepy tropic harbours in mangroved estuaries where the luggers once thronged, and the *bêche-de-mer* boats, before Mikimoto took over with his cultured pearls, and revolutionary days in Asia's politics blighted the Chinese gourmet's delight in the sea slug. These things happen and other things take up; a new industry is established in the district, developing patterns of decentralisation offer different jobs for the young people. Some country towns fade and wither, and others grow and thrive.

As the land becomes increasingly productive and cities grow bigger, the number of people living on the land grows proportionately smaller. Fewer than two of Australia's eleven million are now classified as rural dwellers; more than one-third of the continent, over 720 million acres of it, remains outside the fences of the rural holdings. Most of the still unexploited land lies in Western Australia, South Australia, and the Northern Territory. Large areas are reservations; much of it is desert. Mineral development rather than agriculture is likely to shape its future, and the future dynamism of rural development will be generated in the cities.

The Australian "bush" has never been richer or more productive than it is today. The country supports more stock than ever in its history, the paddocks throw a fatter yield. But the patterns of human settlement have changed from the old ways, and beyond any chance of repetition, almost beyond recognition. The outlines of outback Camelot blur into the fuzz of history. Dad and Dave are memories, as are sundowners at the evening sliprails, bowyangs around ragged moleskin trousers, the snip of shears in the woolsheds, the squeak of buggy springs and the gravelled clatter of iron-rimmed waggon wheels, the stark spectral forests of ring-barked eucalypts. All the yesterdays. And only yesterday, the longer, harder times that built the Australia of today.

THERE ARE YOUNG ONES, too, among the true bush people. They royster down for rodeos and round-ups and riding in the picnic race meetings of the bush. But they also listen to the oldtimers, respecting them for their wisdom of water and survival.

On the famous Birdsville Track, the old stock route down from the Diamantina channel country in south-west Queensland to the Marree railhead which is the gateway to Adelaide, there are 200 miles without surface water. The Simpson Desert is just out there, and it's wise to know where the bores are. The year before last a family of five British migrants lost their bearings and perished on the Track.

There was an oldtimer we ran into, he must have been over 80, and he remembered the boom days of Birdsville, when its population was nearly 400 and there were three pubs open and everyone went around armed because of brawls and sheep-stealers and cattle duffers. He was scornful that only one pub had survived and the population had dropped to about 80, mostly blacks, and they were out now looking for oil in the cattle lands. There was even, he said, talk of a tourist road in place of the Track.

They are growing fewer, the quiet strong men of the big distances, and they like to stay out among the brumby herds and the wild pigs and donkeys, where the lost cattle stray; they leave their messages to each other, and their ribald commentaries on foremen and station bosses,

RIGHT) Sheep drover, Queensland-New South Wales border.

scrawled in picturesque *graffiti* on the bore tanks that mark the long stock routes . . . .

We were camped at Tea Tree Well, and there was that feeling of absolute emptiness, unutterably lonely. Then, riding down the silence, a convoy of trucks came up "the bitumen" from Barrow Creek, such a mechanical clatter in the primal stillness. A night later, on the Katherine, a black stockman, mission-trained, came out of the darkness through wraiths of trees, singing *The Rose of Tralee* . . . .

Cattle station, Cape York Peninsula, northern Queensland.

In an outback pub I stopped with a friend once, for luncheon. The choice was corned beef, and we were each given a dry, coarse, stringy hunk of it. "Vegetables?" my friend asked, and was scornfully reminded of the drought. "Perhaps some tomato ketchup," he tried. She turned to her husband in disgust. "Chuck us over the Red Ned, will you, Ern?" she called. "Bastard 'ere thinks it's Christmas."
Will we ever, I wonder, think of this land as a place for festivals and thanksgivings . . . ?

Every Australian carries around with him the fossil imprints of an earlier past, a reverse image really, of the dead inanimate land embedded

Birdsville Pub at noon, Birdsville, south-west Queensland.

Radio Telephone
COARSE
TUNING
RECEIVER
VOLUME

in the living. You see this most clearly, I think, in the bush people, the outback people, who are the matrix of this mark that is on all of us. There is much beauty and splendour in their faces, and hands. Severe, gaunt and Gothic at times, it is yet softened by a more intimate understanding of that human loneliness that is common to us all. I suppose to understand the distances between people is to value more deeply closeness and sharing.

All the pasts of a countryside are collectively still there, the preserved record of small grandeurs . . . .

It is of Old Ryan, Old Pat, that they talk, remembering the strength and sinew of his brawny, clanging days. On the lot across from the stock and station agent's a weedy patch of onion grass, dandelions and lantana

LEFT) Mother and daughter, Radio School of the Air class, Witchelina Station, South Australia.
RIGHT) Outback station, Angas Downs, Northern Territory.

away from them the simple role and pattern of their being we have the choice of assimilating them into our patterns or finding new ones in which they can share the dignities of work and life. It is no longer enough for us to find casual substitutes which will quieten our guilts, soothe our prides, and satisfy our deepest yearnings for the common man's equalities. These people belong here. They have belonged longer. If it is our land now it was theirs alone through all the long marching days of humanity's journey to civilisation. When the man and woman from whom we are descended were caught in a web of wonder at the usages of flint and digging-stick, in the long dawning ages before Ur and Jericho, these, after all, were the only Australians . . . .

LEFT) Station hand, Brunnette Downs, Northern Territory.
BELOW) Sign at petrol station, Kalbar, Queensland.

Whether in the distances of the Outback or closer to the civilising amenities of the country towns, the rural festivals are the notches of the year, adding pattern to a life that derives its comfort from fixed rhythms. And there is a poetry in this recurrent pageantry of stock sales and agricultural shows, bush races and picnic meetings, which are the punctuations of the rural story.

In the bigger towns and the great coastal cities, the festivals are huge, rich agricultural state fairs of the land, invading steel and concrete worlds with their carnival of ribboned thoroughbreds and rams, bulls and milkers; there are pampered sows and sheepdogs of remarkable sagacity, horsemen and axemen and all the brown men with distance in their eyes.

With these have always come the giant pumpkins and Arab stallions, the pinwheels, candy floss and sideshows, bareback riders and belly dancers and challenging pugilists in coloured tents. The cornucopia of a continent

Horse buyers at yearling sales, Melbourne, Victoria.

is emptied among ferris wheels, Walls of Death, tattooed ladies and Wild Men from Borneo . . . .

On a Queensland road west of the old warrened Anakie gemfields, I once saw three dusty elephants and a caged tiger travelling, an intrusion into the massive presence of the land which was as improbable and brave as any Hannibal's . . . .

Newer times are upon us; there are television towers in the landscape and changing tastes among the country people. The dated little enterprises, those movable feasts of a continent's hinterland, are being forced further and further into the back country. The times are intruding on, and will someday obliterate many of the slow and gentle rhythms of country living, where townspeople envy local sheep owners for imagined wealth, where curtains twitch and gossip has an easy gait, reputation can ride precariously on the thin edge of prejudice, and like the biblical sparrow

LEFT) Civic Theatre, Wagga Wagga, New South Wales.
RIGHT) Saturday morning shopping, Main Street, Griffith, New South Wales.

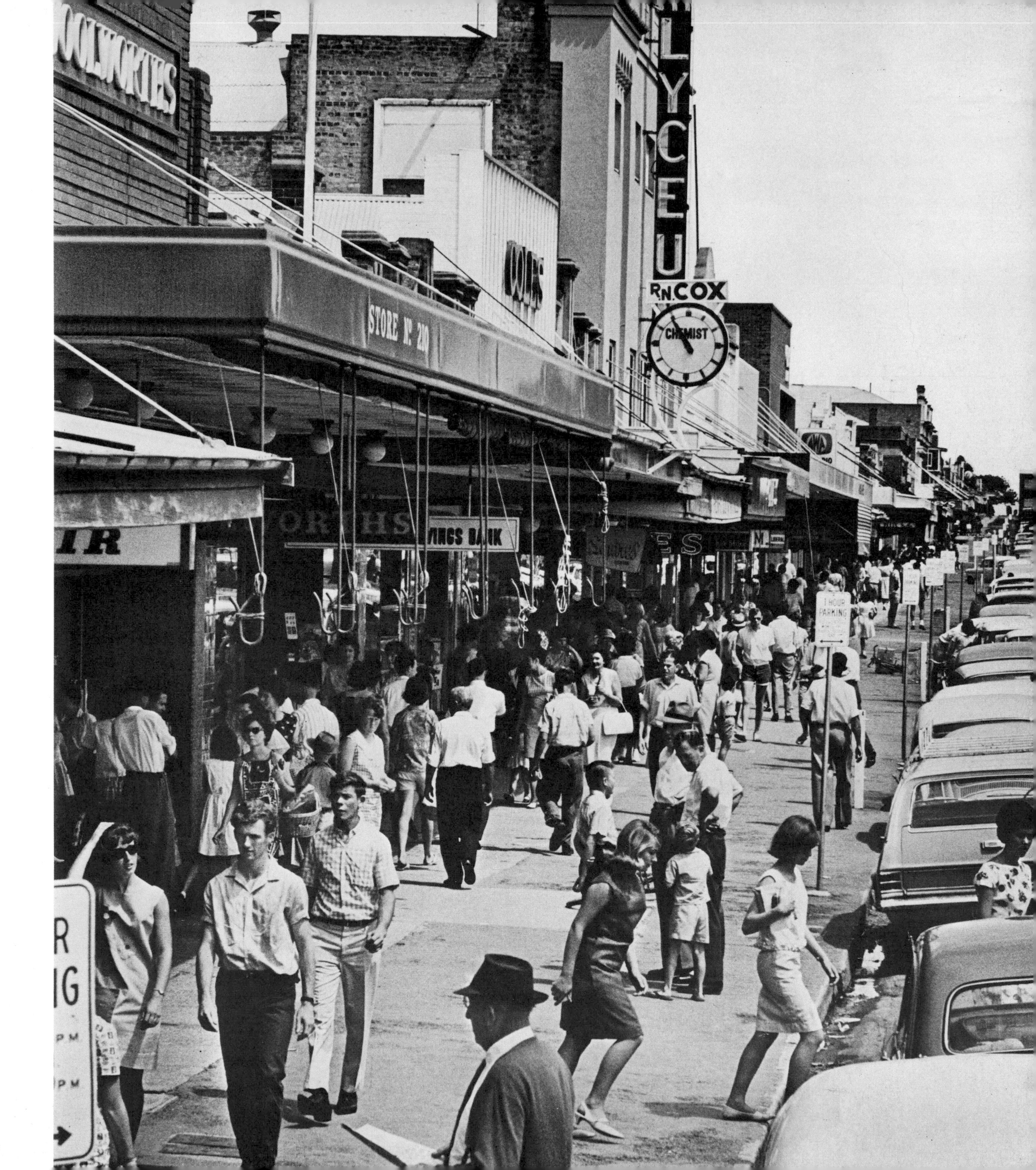

LYCEU
RN.COX
CHEMIST
STORE Nº 210
VINGS BANK
1 HOUR PARKING

no local girl will fall unheeded, where the whole district will give up its week-ends to harvest a sick farmer's crop or build a scout hall for the local kids . . . .

In the Mungle scrub country out of Goondiwindi, they still talk of Stan Bischoff as the nonpareil among scrub gallopers. Even though Stan has been gone from there for years he is part of the history of that district. His father had been a horse-breaker and his mother a shepherd girl on Dangar's big Yallaroi Station when Dangars ran their own wool clippers, lovely square-rigged ships and one of them called the *Yallaroi*, round the Horn and home to London.

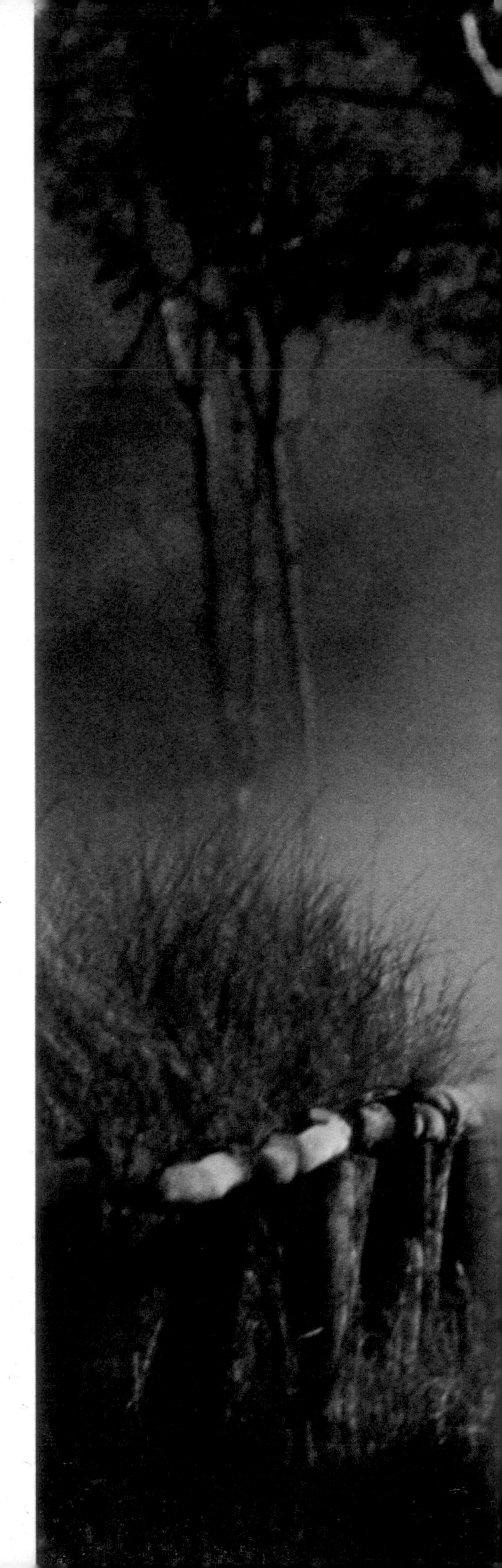

LEFT) Spectators, Laura Picnic Race Meeting, Laura, Queensland.
RIGHT) Annual "grass-fed" bush race meeting, Laura.

When Stan was born on the station the Mungle was the worst scrub in all Australia, belar and brigalow, wilga, whipsticks and thorny wait-a-whiles and a jungle of prickly pear down from the overgrown Billa Billa homestead. But Stan Bischoff could ride muster at full gallop through that tangle where a man afoot would never find a trail, and throw and tie a scrub bull single-handed. The pear has gone and much of the Mungle has been tamed, but Stan Bischoff is still a man of the local epic. The cities would never have known him . . . .

I do not think this is a land that will ever really fill up with people. The cities will crowd and sprawl, and everywhere there will be more people and a gradual shrinking of the massive distances. But always, in much of it, there will remain this feeling of man solitary in the great space.

So in the end we shall have – if we do not already have – this dual image of ourselves, a schizophrenia of cities and the land. And then I suppose we shall have to go out, like pilgrims in a ritual, in search of our other selves, and the earth and sky, rain and drought, survival and death and fire and ashes, that are all part of us. The lucky among us will always be able to find the ritual in our own experience.

Station hands and townspeople, after the races, Laura.

The Cities

With a large continent all to himself, the Australian is by and large a retired Odysseus. He may still like to see himself as "the typical Aussie" – a tall, tough, brown, sinewy man of lean, beaky countenance and narrow buttocks, laconic with his mates, sitting loosely in the saddle and looking out across spinifex and mulga through narrow, sun-creased eyes. Unconsciously, much of his mental outlook and many of his social mannerisms are structured by this illusioned image of himself. But his spectacles have bifocal lenses, and he has taken up squash or ten-pin bowling at his club to get down that little pot that is softening his midriff. Perhaps the most astonishing single fact about the Australian is that in a land with so much room in which to shift around, well over half the population has not moved, in 178 years, farther than a day's march from where the first settlements were established. Australia's little more than eleven million people occupy the same space into which Europe crams 400 million and the United States 190 million.

If all the Australians decided to revert to a simple patriarchal tribal state, and the country's rural stock and holdings were shared out equally, adult Australian males would each own 384 acres of land, a flock of 56 sheep and six head of cattle. This is a rich bounty by any criteria of human history, and even by the standards of most of the contemporary world. But we do not live in tribal patriarchies, life is no longer simple, nomadism is the commodity of the travel agencies, and Australia is urban. More than six million of her people live in the same six coastal cities where colonisation began. And more than half of these – 4,300,000 of them – live in only two cities, Sydney and Melbourne.

To a great degree population has clustered where the rain falls, in a thin and almost unbroken coastal crescent stretching from Cairns in the tropical north-east to Adelaide in the south, a distance of nearly 3,000 miles. The crescent is often only a mile or so wide, seldom more than 20 to 25 miles wide. Within this narrow strip are Australia's four largest cities, Sydney, Melbourne, Brisbane and Adelaide. Westward from Adelaide the great gap of over a thousand miles of bleak desert or near-desert separates Perth, the fifth of the major cities, from the urbanised east. Five of the six State capitals, Sydney, Melbourne, Adelaide, Perth and Hobart, lie enviably in the Antipodean equivalent of Mediterranean latitudes.

Customs, costume and patterns of living are to a great degree informally standardised in all Australian cities. The Australian himself, pretty much at home wherever he happens to be in his own country, is inclined to equate city differences with the comparative merits of the beer more than with civic standards or the character of the people. And if not by beer then by how much the rain falls, or the state of the traffic congestion, by variations in the laws controlling liquor or gambling, by the "softness" or "hardness" of the public water supply (in an Adelaide bar a customer can ask for Melbourne water in his Scotch and get it), by the courtesy or lack of it displayed by motorists, by whether the firemen wear brass helmets or plastics ones, by the prettiness or smartness of the girls, by which code of football is played. Bandinage, conversation, attitudes, even the mordant warnings against asking for credit printed in hotel bars, are unvarying throughout the country. There are more distinct variations in life in England's clustered Home Counties than in the whole vastness of Australia.

The distinction of Australian cities is almost never a physical thing. Only Sydney, with its superb harbour, is able to challenge on merit of pure physical beauty the loveliest seaports of the world. Generally speaking Australian cities are at another disadvantage. Too young to have developed their own accretions of traditional culture or exotic custom, they lack the historical stratification of cities of the older world. Even a "colonial" architecture is not easy to find and, when found, turns out to be transplanted, often vandalised, and only lately respected. No truly indigenous Australian architecture has yet appeared – although the land cries out for an inspired originator – and cities are inclined to present a hodgepodge of imitations and importations. Recently, however, some of it has been good, and hopefully, a little of it very good. The Sydney Opera House, for example, presently maligned in some circles for its excessive cost, is likely in five hundred years' time still to be one of the great architectural triumphs of the Twentieth Century. But there is a curious and disquieting *sameness* that pervades all Australian cities, even when some are planned, like Melbourne and Adelaide, and some, like hilly Sydney and insouciant Perth, seem to grow organically from the run of tidal inlets or the meandering tracks of the old bullock drays.

In part, this is because the Australian city exists as a core, with life radiating out of it to the near-by beaches or bush or hills. For all their easy informality – business deals can be settled without a contract in a pub over schooners of beer – Australian cities can be a frantic tumult during the daytime hours of office work and business. Parking police are active, traffic police implacable, and in the vast cornucopia empires of the department stores shopping matrons wearing astonishing hats ride tireless escalators like swans in *Lohengrin*. But at dusk, when a European city burgeons into the flavoursome fulfilment of the day, Australians hurry home. The city languishes under the dark, star-scattered night, the opacity of its windowed eyes fixed blankly on the fuss and fume of neon. At week-ends it hibernates. The truth is that most Australians are not really urban at all, but *sub*urban, and the city dweller, bustling and bustled as he might be, very often works not for the ambition of "getting to the top," but simply to achieve private dominion of his suburban plot and the freedom of his week-ends and holidays.

All this has the effect of imparting a kind of schizophrenic quality to everyday existence. There is, on one hand, the world of the office or shop or factory, and on the other the world of the home with its integrated entertainments and relaxations. A brief amalgam of a sort may, indeed often does, occur in a pub after work; but otherwise the two worlds seldom impinge on one another. The woman's world is her own pleasant and comfortable domestic kingdom – in which, more often than not, she is still enshrined as "Mum" or "the wife" or "the old girl," and it is there she stays, sharing little with her husband beyond simple domestic felicities. Entertainment is generally *in* the home, and usually involves small fixed coteries of long standing and familiar, therefore agreeable habits, friends and opinions. If this schizophrenia has its drawbacks from a national standpoint – and more than a few of Australia's European immigrants have migrated back home in bored bewilderment at Australian cities' lack of nocturnal fellowship – it does reflect a comfortable prosperity which is more widespread and more evenly distributed than in any other country on the face of the earth.

What this low-order homing instinct results in is sprawl. Sprawl is the consistent characteristic of the Australian cities and no one who has seen them, particularly Sydney and Melbourne, can doubt the Australians' determination to find some use for all that space. Cranes high on fretted skylines are the symbols of a new metropolitan Australia, but beyond horizon-rim stretch the russet plains of suburbia. Red tiles mostly and red brick, ranging from the ruddy through the liverish to the apoplectic, they are depressing under the bright revealing sun, although some alchemy of the Australian light and atmosphere can transform them into a magical fairyland of jewelled splendour when seen by night from an aircraft. This is territory vehemently possessed. *Per capita*, the Australian is the world's most substantial owner of private housing and he accepts without complaint his crowded, hour-long journey to work by bus or train, or the infuriating lunacy of peak-hour motoring, if it entitles him to his own little private dominion around his domestic walls. Although gregarious by nature, he is not one for outright cheek-by-jowl living; there must be a division, however narrow, from his neighbour's property. A lawn and a few shrubs, flower gardens, borders, probably a barbecue pit, possibly a plaster gnome, sometimes a patio, occasionally a swimming pool, his own trees, often a little patch of genuine bushland loud with birds. And fenced in, of course. He likes to be fenced in. Nowhere in the world is there so much domestic living space so democratically shared, nor so jealously cared for. And so the sprawl spreads further.

The molecular unit of sprawl is the five-roomed house. As architect and critic Robin Boyd has written: "The Australian town-dweller spent a century in the acquisition of his toy: an emasculated garden, a five-roomed cottage of his very own, different from its neighbours by a minor contortion of window or porch – its difference significant to no one but himself. He skimped and saved for it, and fought two World Wars with it figuring prominently in the back of his mind. Whenever an Australian boy spoke to an Australian girl of marriage, he meant, and she understood him to mean, a life in a five-roomed house." The extent to which these molecules are multiplied is indicated by some rather startling statistics from a recent census. At that counting 93.5 per cent of Sydney's inhabitants lived outside the municipality of Sydney; and 92 per cent of Melbourne's inhabitants lived in the vast rings of suburbs outside the city.

There are critics who condemn this city-suburban life as humdrum, insular and complacent, but in modern life it is very unwise to lay down rules. If the Australian has never again tried to push inland, it may well be because he has everything he wants right where he is.

His cities are orderly and on the whole clean, efficient and benevolent. They have skies as well as skylines. There are no true slums, no real poverty; a recent survey showed that the earnings of the average family in Sydney were 84 Australian dollars per week. The Australian is not familiar with the smell of city violence. He lacks experience of racial rioting or looting. He has not known the bombs and barricades and armed militia of Europe's streets, nor the menacing hostility of the New York parks. When a record haul of $200,000 worth of contraband heroin and opium was seized on an Asiatic freighter in Sydney Harbour last year it was automatically and naturally assumed that the illicit drugs were on their way to the U.S.A., since, as the Customs official said, "There is practically no demand for the drug heroin in Australia."

People are friendly in the shops, and the market stalls display breathtaking evidence of nature's bounty and fecundity. The fruit is fabulous, the steaks a dream for he-men, the oysters, the crayfish, the huge pink prawns matchless, the beer is the best and strongest in the world. Thanks to the coming of the immigrants in their post-war hundreds of thousands, a world's cuisine is now offered in the restaurants and a new cosmopolitanism spices the cores of Australia's cities.

In such a world if the pulse of living extends outwards from the city proper to simplified, perhaps even unsophisticated, but certainly uncomplicated patterns of recreation, of escape, of amusement, under a high blue sky and a warm sun, who's the loser? The suburban or the roadside pub, the backyard barbecue, sportsfields everywhere, the race tracks, the wealth of splendid public beaches unfouled by the rapacity of concessionaires, and the green lungs of the public parks – all these abound. Much can be said for the simplicity of the Australian's pleasures.

Of Australian cities, Sydney is the oldest and the largest (founded 1788; population 2,300,000). By standard measurements it is only about 40th among world cities, but by its personality and character it has to be numbered among the world's dozen "great" cities. Quintessentially an oceanic city, Sydney has some of the swagger and boisterousness of a sailor ashore, and it doesn't take long to call you by your first name. Its luck is that it has never succeeded entirely in desecrating the superb beauty of its natural setting. It sprawls everywhere around the magnificence of its great deepwater harbour and the many tentacles of its river inlets and secret bays and islands. Small craft and yachts with coloured spinnakers sail like flocks of humming-birds beneath foreshore apartment blocks, and there is no other city that can offer within its own suburbs three hundred miles of municipal boundaries which are defined by beaches, ocean cliffs, river banks, islands and tidal shores. There are 22 magnificent ocean surf beaches only a walk or a short bus ride away for millions of city dwellers.

Sydney is also the city which has given birth to the new phenomenon of the social clubs. These suburban centres – sometimes huge and lavish, usually very wealthy – are to the ordinary family much more than the Country Club used to be to the wealthy businessman. They are a kind of package deal of an earlier home life, when people had both less leisure and less distraction; they are the first collectivisation of suburban simplicities plus a good many other conveniently packaged things – an apotheosis of the English pub, repositories of mass social culture where simply *everything* is available – a gambling flutter at the poker machines, a sociable game of euchre or bowls, a Continental meal or a comradely dance, an uplifting orchestral concert, a title match between professional pugilists, an informative lecture. Club life is still too young and not yet widespread enough for one to judge its ultimate effects on Australian *mores*, but it is already an important social phenomenon.

Melbourne (founded 1835; population 2,000,000 plus) is still far more inclined to rely for relaxation on old-fashioned "entertainment in the home." Of all Australian cities, the two giants, Sydney and Melbourne, are the least like each other, and a longstanding and potent rivalry continues to flourish between them. The stereotype beloved by most Melburnians, is that Sydney is noisy, garish, untidy, pushing, callous, glossy in life and cold-blooded in business, insincere, brash, rather delinquent, and on the whole untrustworthy. The same Melburnians consider themselves quiet, well-mannered, industrious, perhaps a little over-reticent and reserved, but not really cold, a thoughtful people, fond of music and theatre and "keen on" culture, great ones for the home, and with a remarkable flair for fashion, particularly among the women.

Melbourne's insularity has contributed to the development of powerful forces that should not be underrated. If Sydney has achieved that essential quality of the great city – that it minds its own business – Melbourne has become the intellectual forcing-house of the land. There is a saying that Melbourne creates the ideas and Sydney carries them out; there is just enough truth in this to make one hesitate before challenging. Certainly Melbourne germinates a disproportionate share of the country's forces, often for culture and scholarship, but more usually for finance, commerce, public taste and Government. It is growing faster, and, in the end, might well become the dominant city in Australia.

Yet Melbourne was founded, somewhat illegally, by free settlers 47 years after the Sydney colony was established. The way to this latter-day Promised Land was shown by two businessmen who astutely bartered blankets, beads and other traditional trade goods with the Yarra aborigines for 600,000 acres. One of them, John Batman, said, "This will be the place for a village." Sydneysiders enjoy recalling this remark, and add, "How right he was."

The American actress Ava Gardner, when she was working in Melbourne on the film of Australian Nevil Shute's book, *On The Beach*, was widely quoted as saying: "What a perfect place to make a movie about the end of the world."

In all its infancy Melbourne resisted all efforts to have it made a convict settlement, and, with Adelaide, prides itself on being free from what used to be called "the taint." Aside from a mad, uninhibited, rambunctious, rampaging spree during the gold rushes, it followed a dour, energetic, generally Presbyterian pattern of progress. When the separate colonies federated into one commonwealth nation at the beginning of this century, it seemed the most natural thing in the world that Melbourne, then Australia's biggest city, should become the interim capital. It was already the vice-regal seat, the heart of banking, commerce, and industry, the defence centre and the spiritual leader of the young nation. Once the capital shifted to Canberra, however, some balance was restored between the two rivals.

Sydney and Melbourne are in agreement about the other cities. Brisbane (founded 1824; population 635,000) is relaxed, friendly, easy-going, more an overgrown town than a city. Suburban gardens blaze with bougainvillia, hibiscus, frangipani, flame-tree, azalea and poinsettia. Businessmen wear shorts, sandals and shirtsleeves, and business deals are usually made slowly over beer in cool bars. In spite of a lavish town hall of which the inhabitants are inordinately proud – it spreads two-and-a-half acres of pseudo-Renaissance architecture over the town's original waterhole – a countrified atmosphere lingers on. The wide verandas on their slender posts, as much as the men in their broad-brimmed hats and elastic-sided boots, hint at the vastness of the Queensland bush beyond.

Adelaide (founded 1836; population 600,000), beneath its deceptively staid exterior, for some years has been quietly developing not only into a small city of very considerable charm but into a cultural and commercial centre of great significance to the country as a whole. Its biennial Festival of Arts is now recognised internationally. Like Edinburgh, it is a city of perfect size, ideal harmony, and has precisely the right *feel* for this sort of festival.

The only truly planned city among the earlier colonial centres (Adelaide people, who have the best sense of humour in Australia, like to say "We're well laid out because we've been dead so long"), Adelaide has beautiful streets, miles of parklands, a splendid setting and a fine climate, and some of the most charming colonial architecture in the land. With the strong European migration to South Australia, especially to the vineyards and dried fruit areas, this part of Australia is developing a very special character of its own. The people are neither as reserved as Melburnians nor as gregarious as Sydney-siders. Although tolerant and good-humoured, they are more complicated and more energetic than the easy-going Queenslanders. At Festival time their whole city comes alive with a warm-blooded exuberance that is quite Mediterranean in feeling.

To reach Perth (founded 1829; population 450,000) from other centres of urban society, Australians must cross miles of desert and nightmarish salt lake country, and the magnificently desolate Nullarbor Plain. In spite of its size and isolation, the capital of the gigantic empty State of Western Australia is many Australians' favourite city. It fulfills the basic requirement of brewing a very creditable beer. It really *does* have a Mediterranean climate; with a year-round daily average of just under eight hours of sunshine, it is the continent's sunniest capital. Many people also think it is the prettiest. It is by any odds the friendliest. And it is usually conceded that Perth girls are the country's most attractive.

But the soul and heart of this excellent little city on the delightful estuary named after the black swan is a sense of excitement, even heady exhilaration. For inland lies Western Australia, where the greatest battle for the land is being fought. There in the Esperance Basin, Americans are developing millions of acres for sale to Australian farmers. There in the north are Arizona rice growers, and Texans buying into the cattle runs. There French engineers plan mighty power installations driven by 35-foot tides. And there on North West Cape is the giant U.S. communications centre, and at Carnarvon the great N.A.S.A. space-tracking station. The West has all the basic Australian problems, presented on the largest scale – the vast stretch of distance and virtually no water, some of the world's bleakest deserts: not enough people, not enough money – and an immense potential. It is the West of all the Horace Greeleys, and Perth feeds on it, and is touched by it.

The island state of Tasmania is frequently and carelessly dropped off maps, and many people abroad genuinely believe Tasmania to be a quite separate country from Australia. The people of Hobart (established 1804; population 117,000) sometimes think this themselves. In fact, with its running streams and stone bridges, its hedged lanes and hamlets set in green and tranquil landscapes, its patterned orchards, snow slopes and dark forests, the island seems to have a closer affinity with England or New England than with the huge brown continent standing across Bass Strait. Hobart itself sharpens the illusion.

It is the sea that flavours Hobart. The city has a smell of Whitby or Yarmouth or one of the Cornish seaports. With its cobbled streets and old stone lofts and warehouses and the salty run of its quays, with its still-lingering atmosphere of convict ships and whalers, immigrant packets and the famous Hobart clippers, it could even be Salem or New Bedford. Tasmania was the last part of Australia to relinquish sail, and even then bowed to progress reluctantly. Whaling ships still put in to Hobart Town to bring back the old smell that Herman Melville knew; and explorers' ships still put out of there to sail past lonely Maatsuyker Island, the southernmost tip of Australia, and thence south across the cold heaving wastes to the Antarctic Continent.

A place of ample rainfall and of rushing streams, Tasmania is rapidly becoming one of the tourist centres of the country. Here are vast still forests, almost impenetrable and some to this day unexplored, the awesome and sinister ruins of the convict settlement at Port Arthur, the "Devil's Island" of the bad old days. But here also is all the thriving energy of the Twentieth Century – great hydroelectric schemes, copper smelters, alumina refineries, timber mills, the heart of the nation's paper industry. Green Tasmania is different from the rest of Australia, as Hobart is different from all other capital cities.

Canberra, the national capital, is different too, but in another way. Where the other cities have grown out of the last century or the century before, Canberra (established 1911; population 70,000 plus) was created and implanted squarely in this century. It is the baby of Australian cities – and a product of artificial insemination, at that – the brainchild of Frank Lloyd Wright's disciple, W. Burley Griffin, of Chicago, who won an international competition in 1912 to plan the new capital. His far-sighted vision is only now becoming visible in its full character and maturity. But there is a vivacity and an excitement there now that few other Australian cities can challenge. For Canberra crystallises so many of the facets of today's Australia; the city of Australia's national parliament it flashes the brilliant colours of ceremony and governmental panoply, of academic robes and a new world of science, of the world's embassies and all their people, of a nation's history epitomised by the quietness of people in their gardens. Once regarded as dull and bureaucratic, Canberra grows livelier in the Australian scene, sparkling in its intellectual ambitions as well as its spectacular setting of spring blossoms or the rich, imported tonings of northern autumn.

These, then, are the Australian cities. There are other towns which are big enough to be cities, but aren't; or which should be cities but aren't big enough. Wollongong, 40 miles south of Sydney, and the centre of the Illawara cattle and farming district, and the coal and steel port of Newcastle, 100 miles north-east of Sydney and at the mouth of the Hunter River, each have a population approaching 150,000. Yet neither has developed the individual personality or characterful city centre to make it more than a dark spot on a map showing population or industrial density; they are satellite cities of the sprawling Sydney megalopolis. The brave little government town of Alice Springs, closest of all to the centre of the continent, and tropical, flavoursome Darwin, with one of the finest harbours in the world and the most polyglot of Australia's populations, have the character to enrich the nation, but remain locked from growth by the brown land's forbidding geography, while more and more of the lean, brown men with the hawk beaks and narrow buttocks crowd into the five-roomed cottages along the south-eastern coastal crescent of the continent.

Most of the Australians are now faces in all these streets and the most familiar sights of Australia become cranes on a skyline and a couple in the candlelit jazz cellar, a man tending his garden or browsing in a bookshop; balloons of cheese in an Italian delicatessen, the world of the garden party, the young and old together, lovers in doorways, the spilling cornucopias of the market stalls, the rivers of colour flowing in suburban streets where the girls in high-school uniforms wait for after-school buses; the glimpse through a cottage window of a Greek family before an icon, the flourish of a waiter's hand; a child and a dog racing for a ball.

For all these things are cities, and Australians have become city people.

THE LUNCHTIME OFFICE HOUR is the time for a stranger to look at the Australian city. Here, below the high cranes in minuet on new clear skylines, flow the faces in the streets, the element of surprise and chance encounter, and that daily expectancy of unprecedented adventures which is any city's bonus gift. Here are entertainments formal and fortuitous, and the crisp and clashing clangour of human activities, Breughel-rich to the eye of the perceptive, and the hurrying young in the seducible arrogance of their vital, healthy, brown-skinned well-being.

On city corners clerks and office workers eat from brown paper bags luncheon sandwiches and meat pies adrip with sanguinary ketchup; window-shopping matrons in splendid hats chew potato crisps or lick at ice-creams, and the young and old sprawl in turfy parks to listen to symphonic music. Crowded pubs overspill to bustling pavements short-sleeved, beer-sipping men who talk of cricket scores and racetracks and watch with eyes of tentative judgement the upright, high-stepping girls go by . . . .

There is nothing in the world quite like an Australian city, except every other Australian city. Climates differ, so do surface values; but the family likenesses are unmistakable. Cities, of course, are people. And in Australian cities people dress, talk, saunter, obey, lounge, loll, drink, woo and walk like each other and at the same time like nobody anywhere else in the world.

The simplest of generalisations is that Australians and Americans are the two most instantly identifiable peoples of the western world. After ten years of living in Europe I could on a Mediterranean waterfront unerringly recognise from 150 yards away an Australian arriving on the noonday steamer. When I returned to my native land I had been absent for more than fourteen years. Yet everywhere I looked they were the same people I had recognised from that quayside, but infinitely

Lunch hour, Hyde Park, downtown Sydney.

THE
RAIN!
AREAS
1ST. TEST
TRIALS
MOBILISED
ESCORT

multiplied. The first vivid impressions of that homecoming I have not had reason to change . . . .

Able to live without the gift of seasons or the sting of natural hazards, the urban Australian contrives simplicities to offset the stressful demands a city makes. His cities have the graceful accident of sunlight and release, but have acquired or preserved few mysteries. They show no evidence of grim and greedy yesterdays, no emanations of outcast pasts. These seem to have been scoured by fresh air and scrubbed away by the white sun. Sunlight spreads into the old chinks and crannies, and the salted air blows in from the bright sea.

We like things to be above board and communicable. We live by

---

LEFT) Western suburbs from the air, Sydney.
RIGHT) Young Australians, North Avalon Beach, New South Wales.

conventional decencies and plausible gains, we shun affectations and mistrust the eccentrics; and among ourselves we seem a comfortable, friendly, unhurried, law-abiding and highly democratic people. No cities in the world are as casual and easy-going as ours, none as evenly spread with the good life.

We are uncomfortable only with the stranger who seems not really to understand the worthiness we see in our simplifications, who seems to have known streets still haunted by gloomy ghosts, where the shadows are not dispelled by our bright sun, or sent dancing by our clean sea winds. And we are inclined to frown on any undertones of darker mysteries in ourselves, in our mates,

LEFT) Evening rush hour, Circular Quay, Sydney.
BELOW) Roadside sign approaching Surfer's Paradise, Queensland.

PEARL

in our womenfolk, in our cities and in our place in the sun. For most of us, the bright and the *new* are quite sufficient . . . .

To Suit Every Purse and Need, says the hoarding within the sputtering ice-blue frame of neon. Sparkling wines and lotteries. Lubricants and lay-bys. To Suit Every Purse and Need. The urban Australian believes firmly and unhypocritically in the acquisition of the good things of life. And he has his own definite opinion of what the good things are. Usually he is trying to answer an inner rather than a competitive urge.

LEFT) Downtown Sydney from the air.
RIGHT) Melbournites waiting for the "Moomba Festival" parade.

His hedonism is real, but not too complicated. His pubs are there to sell beer, not to provide "cosiness" or "sophistication." It's the best beer in the world, isn't it? What more do you want . . . ?

But it is one thing to be carefree and another to be careless. There is a good deal of talk these days about "the visual environment" of the Australian – what he has done and is doing to it, and what he plans to do about it. With such easy access to a splendour of beaches and so much sunny space available to ordinary suburban people, there is much to be said for not allowing ambitions to outweigh the simpler pleasures of living. Yet more and more Australians are becoming agitated

RIGHT) Free public concert, Myer Music Bowl, Melbourne.

LADIES
GENTS

about wild and tasteless depredations in and around their cities.

Still we like to leave the worrying to politicians and planners; we forget they like to be carefree too. Worse, we pass the buck to "developers" who are carefree in an entirely different way. They may not have succeeded in subjugating our continent yet, but they certainly can make a subdivision look silly.

If the concern about this grows and spreads, it might not yet be too late. But ordinary people will have to look up from the beds of zinnias they tend

---

LEFT) Camping area, Burleigh Heads Beach, southern Queensland.
BELOW) Sign, Surfer's Paradise, Queensland.
RIGHT) Homeowner, Surfer's Paradise.

with such sedulous private worship and look around at the total landscaping of the cities they inhabit . . . .

Where thought and imagination have been applied there may be a marvellous affinity between the habitations of man and the natural qualities of the Australian environment, a precise harmony that sings like music under the great sky. Here and there one sees it, the hint and promise of the cities of our oncoming future. So we shall have only ourselves to blame if, in the end, the ugliness and not the harmony prevails . . . .

The transformation of the city-living Australian becomes more and more an obsession with the elusive question of "style" and "influences." We like to think of ourselves as a highly individualistic people of intact image, but we are more susceptible than we care to admit to "influences." There is much talk now of "the Continental influence," "the American influence," "the English influence," and, in sum, "the Cosmopolitan Style."

As the tempo of change accelerates, the influences help shape new facets of the Australian character – the higher education and a new nomadic spirit among the younger Australians, the acceptance of some, if not yet enough Continental ideas, a spectrum

---

LEFT) Tennis class, Roseville, Sydney.
RIGHT TOP) Canberra and Lake Burley Griffin from the air, Australian Capital Territory.
RIGHT BOTTOM) Government House garden party, Canberra, in honour of Royal Visit.

of refinements in taste, an admission that the artist or the intellectual can be as important, and as honoured an Australian as the sportsman or the warrior, a growing interest in and respect for our own history . . . .

"I cannot understand this new generation," the stately grey-haired dowager said to me with testy impatience. "Would you believe it; they are even beginning to take up those awful convicts . . . ."

There is more to "Continental influence" than having wine with a meal or cooking with garlic and olive

---

LEFT) Monthly gourmet dinner of the Escoffier Society, Sydney.
BELOW) Refreshment stand, sports ground Perth, Western Australia.

oil or in the land that grows the finest wool on earth buying sweaters from Italy. The trouble is that many of us accept the new influences only so long as they do not affect the old familiar images we have of ourselves. We grow self-conscious rather than sophisticated.

No nation is mature until it has learnt to be self-critical. It is fortunate that there is beginning now within Australia a definite and growing iconoclasm to mix with our conviction that each year here is vintage for our youth. There is even some willingness to accept criticism from the outsider, which used never to be tolerated. So if outwardly the family likeness remains in all the cities, diversification is budding and old smugness being shattered.

LEFT) Week-end surfer, Newport, New South Wales.
RIGHT) Opening night, Her Majesty's Theatre, Melbourne.

SUTHERLAND
GRAND OPERA
OPERA
ZSF·170

Most people live in cities because they like living in cities. This is a plain fact that politicians, economists, demographers, and sociologists can do very little about. So I sympathise with the Victorian cabinet minister who, brooding over the acute housing shortage in his fair city not so long ago, finally wrote to 10,000 applicants for State housing with the quite simple suggestion that they should move to the country. He must have known that his plea would be in vain . . . .

The love of a city, like any love, is of the heart rather than of the mind, and the depth and permanence of that love, like any love, is a sum of memories. I am a city man, bred and by inclination, and I have had the luck to live in many cities –

LEFT AND RIGHT) Lady patrons, Grand Opera opening night, Her Majesty's Theatre, Melbourne.

the cities that are mistresses to men, Paris and Rome, Florence and Athens; the titan cities, New York, Chicago, London, Tokyo; exotic cities like Caracas and Mandalay and Isfahan. Yet I and many like me come back to Sydney with a delight in memories and images that the heart will cherish long after the mind has ceased to carp.

The shadows of the West are on the waters, the homing ferries are aslide on an effulgence of light, the terraced pinnacles of merchandise are aloof above a sheen of liquid colour. A man is fishing from a jetty, a boy seeks limpets in a foreshore rock pool; a keel grates on a shingle, and the great Pacific darkens in empurpled splendour. Here we have lived and loved and sung and walked in private streets, and talked night's candles down to waxy encrustations on discarded bottles. Here we have heard music adrift on many scented evenings, and known friendship.

In any city dreams are to be found as well as nightmares. Often it is our own choice.

LEFT) Evening, inland reaches, Sydney Harbour from the air.

The Mixture

It would be interesting to canvass the Sydney suburb of Matraville to find out how many of the residents know why their place of domicile was so named; or to ascertain how many Australians realise that they are here largely because of the intuition and fervour of a young American.

James Mario Matra, an American-born loyalist, was a 25-year-old midshipman serving on Cook's *Endeavour*. He was so impressed by the eastern seaboard of Australia that in 1783 he printed a monograph, *Proposals for Establishing a Settlement in New South Wales*, which became a powerful influence in the foundation of the first colony. Matra's original plan was to settle the place with Englishmen and exiled American loyalists supplemented by Tahitians, with mistresses provided for the original pioneers; and to establish a centre for trade with the Spice Islands and the Orient, and a base from which to make rollicking raids against the Spaniards and the Dutch. Later talks with Lord Sydney caused him to revise this exotic and adventurous plan and suggest, instead, a penal settlement at Botany Bay. Even here he had excellent ideas which were, unfortunately, not implemented; his plan for reforming the transported convicts was to restore them to their dignity by giving them freehold acres of their own to cultivate.

By the time Matra died in his early sixties in 1806 the Australian colonies had become, in fact, an extension of the British Isles. They were immensely far removed, it is true, and strangely and starkly environed, but certainly not gummed up with any Polynesian nonsense of grass skirts and bare breasts, or uncalled for pugnacities against the Dutch and French, or communistic ideas of sharing the land with felons, or officially condoned licentiousness, or any other newfangled humbug. Mother England was in charge, and Mother England intended to stay in charge. And for a very long time, in greater or lesser degree, she did.

The relationship, it is true, was never one of constant, clear-cut issues. The child grew into a sturdy and sometimes self-willed adult; there were times when he was the incorrigibly bad boy of the Imperial family, other briefer times when he was the well-beloved son. Yet British the place unquestionably remained: the Queen of England continues to be the Queen of Australia, Governors-General come and go in her name, the Union Jack is still hoisted, the National Anthem is still the old anthem of the old empire. Australian volunteers for England's war of 1914–18 suffered proportionately the heaviest casualties of any nation involved. And until quite recently most Australians were inordinately proud that their 97 per cent British racial stock made them slightly more British than the homeland British themselves. Some, and perhaps all of these things are in a process of change, and it is very probable that the next twenty years will see a metamorphosis more startling than any happening over the last century and three-quarters. It is significant that when former Prime Minister Sir Robert Menzies said recently, "We're British to our boot heels," he not only spoke the truth but angered most of his countrymen. Already racial purity is down a bit, to around 90 per cent. Although this hardly overspices the concoction the new flavours have a powerful pungency which, as with good spices, is out of all proportion to the quantity used.

Although it was hardly continuous, the seasoning process began with the discovery of gold in 1851 and the free immigration which resulted from it. Gold brought some minor but significant intrusions of Germans, Americans and Chinese to mix with the dominant English, Scots, Irish and Welsh, and a little later, there were Kanaka labourers brought in from the South Sea Islands. The intruders did not bring with them the degree of violence and anarchy which had been anticipated, but they did have a very sharp impact on what had been entirely British attitudes.

The many thousands of American fortune-seekers who took ship across the Pacific from the ports of California were a new sort of man in the colonial world. Individualists and frontiersmen, they were from a young country still involved in the immense dimensions of continental development. They had hard-won convictions about the tenure of the land and made no bones about their feelings toward a privileged "squattocracy." Their exhortations to the colonials to overthrow the Crown fell, in the main, on deaf ears, and some Australians resented their braggadocio. Yet they made a strong impression. Young Australians sedulously copied (as a century later they again copy) their clothes, their slang, their bowie knives and their harness trappings. American-style buggies, gigs and sulkies supplanted the creaking old bullock waggons, and the famous four-wheeled stagecoaches imported in 1853 enabled Cobb and Company to dominate Australia's inland roads for decades. It was the Americans who first gave the "modern touch" to Australian life.

While industrious, unflamboyant Germans were moving unobtrusively through the goldfields into gem-cutting and such little businesses as lithographic printeries, on to small farm selections or slopes where they planted vines from cuttings brought all the way from the Rhine or the Moselle, 40,000 Chinese coolies were causing a problem. Mostly from Canton, brought in during the 'forties and 'fifties as cheap indentured labour, many of them were, in effect, slaves. Their case should have had strong appeal to that colonial mentality so basically concerned with the plight of the underdog. In fact, they were treated abominably, accused of bringing leprosy and smallpox to the colonies, of following heathen practices, of luring white women to their squalid opium dens, and of indulging in unmentionable vices. They were reviled, robbed, stoned, mobbed, murdered and even scalped for the curiosity of their pigtails. The Chinese's only rivals for the bottom rung in Australian life were the Kanakas.

The Kanakas were for the most part Melanesian people from the nearer South Pacific Islands, and they were brought in as indentured labour for the sugar plantations of tropical North Queensland. The theory of the trade was that "white men don't work in the tropics," but by and large it was a traffic carried on by "blackbirding" brigs and schooners. It took fifty years before the Kanaka imports finally ceased altogether in 1904, by which time 57,000 natives had come into Australia.

Although much to do with plain ignorance, the Australian attitude towards the Chinese and the Kanakas had a strong basis in economic fear. In their uncompromising land the Australians saw the struggle for a better way of life as tough enough without foreigners coming in and "living on the smell of an oil rag." The real bogey was "cheap foreign labour" rather than colour prejudice. Thus the earliest union work codes excluded Chinese, Kanakas, Japanese and Afghans, yet accepted American Negroes, New Zealand Maoris and all half-castes born in Australia.

In all, the gold of the 'fifties had caused Australia's population to triple. Newly arrived professional men and skilled craftsmen helped broaden the rigid pattern of colonial ideas. Standards of literacy and education, until then possessed by a privileged few, were extended and raised through the whole social structure. As for the Chinese and Kanakas, quite unwittingly they had succeeded in firmly establishing the principle of "White Australia" in national policy.

With the coming of the Twentieth Century, the separate colonies federated at last into a united nation, and, the threat of cheap foreign labour removed, Australia seemed prepared to proceed pleasantly with the task of keeping itself essentially British.

It was the pinnacle of Imperial glory. A pink flush suffused the map of the world. The established institutions of "Home" were sedulously transplanted. Legal and parliamentary procedures were modelled on the Inns of Court and Whitehall. Cricket became *the* game. Boat races were a good thing. Thoroughbred racehorses were imported from English studs; so, in a slightly different sense, were Governors and Governors-General. Royal birthdays were observed with solemnity, as was Trafalgar Day, St Patrick's Day, St George's Day and even Bobby Burns Day. There was Empire Day for the patriots and Eight Hours Day for the workers, but Australia Day was still the Cinderella among anniversaries.

The hot roast joint and the indigestible hot suet pudding which followed were *de riguer* for Sundays even when the shade temperature stood at 108 degrees; Australia broiled in December heat waves, but Christmas Day meant hot roast turkey and plum pudding with brandy sauce. Tea and beer were the national drinks, not coffee, which was "American," and not wine, which was "European" and usually derided as "plonk." Each year British steamship lines were hard put to cope with tens of thousands of sentimental Australians making the ritual pilgrimage "back Home." It was all a far and curiously forgotten cry from the clanking fetters of convict days and the foetid 'tween-decks of the immigrant packets.

But stones cast into dark waters on the far side of the earth were causing uneasy ripples even in distant Australia. The Great World Depression made Australians uncomfortably aware of their dangerous dependence upon remote factors. Although the gold rush immigrants had by now been assimilated, the Germans had survived internment in World War I, and the rather unnecessary renaming of their placid little towns with patriotic Australian nomenclature, a flood of cheap goods pouring in under the imprint "Made in Japan" revived fears of "cheap foreign labour." Then, as Europe convulsed under fascism, the immigrants came again to Australia, this time as uneasy refugees. The country's legal doors opened to them, but the Europeans found an insular land grown out of touch with the fluxes and flavours of a continent polyglot, cosmopolitan and politically inconsistent. In short, the Europeans came up against all the anomalies of Australia, scattered like burrs in a paddock.

The innate kindliness of the Australian, the habit of human sharing imposed by the inhospitable nature of the country, the ready hand, the open door, all these things were still there. But the average Australian was also puzzled, suspicious and overawed by these swarms of nervous newcomers, with their briefcases, strange long overcoats and thick-soled Continental shoes.

The term "refugee" was promptly and derisively shortened to "reffo," until Parliament eventually outlawed the term. For several years no fair dinkum Australian would carry a briefcase for fear of being mistaken for a European. Mutterings of "cheap foreign labour" spread again and dark accusations of sweated workers in suburban backyard factories run by "the bloody reffos" echoed the nineteenth century tales of the Chinese and their opium dens. Deeply moved by the injustice and suffering in Europe, the Australian offered succour genuinely and generously, and, having made the gesture, had no idea of how to follow it up. He clung defensively to his own kith and kin, and angrily criticised the refugees for sticking together with their own kind. He violently opposed anti-Semitism, but made it abundantly clear that he did not like Jews. Decades of conditioning by such popular ultra-nationalist journals as *The Bulletin* and *Smith's Weekly* had convinced many that the only proper thing to be was an Australian. All other peoples could be loosely fitted, hit or miss, into crisply labelled categories – dagoes, balts, jugos, chows, wogs, boongs, yanks, fritzes and poms (for by now the English were included with the rest). Unable to speak any foreign languages himself – and notoriously inept at mastering them when, infrequently, he tried – the Australian generally resented such a shortcoming in others.

The problem was, in fact, beginning to sort itself out when the outside world exploded even more violently. Europe plunged into the grip of disastrous war, and by the end of another year Australian volunteers were fighting in Europe and Africa, and Japan was battering at the very gates of an Australia that would never be the same again.

"Populate or Perish." This vital phrase began to ring in a wartime Australia newly conscious of its gaping spaces and the attraction they exerted for others. Australia vowed to double her rate of population increase with the end of the war, and eventually to achieve a nation of 20 millions. Inspired by dreams of one of the greatest migration programmes of this or any other century, Australian recruiting officers hurried off to the chaos of post-war Europe. In those desperate years Australia could have found 20 millions willing to come immediately, but the human intake had to be selected, controlled, channelled and supervised if Australia itself was not to be thrown into disastrous confusion by its own pressing problems of post-war reconstruction. By 1951 the main stream of immigration was running, powerful yet controlled and measured, the organised sluice from the immense reservoir dammed up behind: already 170,700 homeless European refugees from a world without visas had found sanctuary; hundreds of thousands more were to follow. Between the end of the war and 1963, the country which had entered the war with only 7,000,000 people absorbed a total of 1,942,402 migrants, and of these well over a million came on free or assisted passages.

This, the largest voluntary and organised movement of people in human history, had a shattering effect on Australia, forcing new values, new standards, new viewpoints, new maturities. Not all the immigrants found the great brown land to their liking. Some of the armadas of the time were two-way – the Australia-bound ships packed with hopeful, wide-eyed migrants of forty different nationalities seeking new lives in the far-away south; the same ships returning to Europe carrying handfuls of disgruntled earlier settlers and creative Australians burdened by too much frustration and despair.

Yet the great experiment succeeded, and continues to succeed beyond expectations. The Australian of the late 'fifties was now wiser, more mature, a more sympathetic figure than the Depression-haunted figure of the 'thirties. The more bigoted aspects of chip-on-the-shoulder nationalism had died with *Smith's Weekly* and only the name of the chauvinistic *Bulletin* was to survive. Prejudice still persisted out of insularity, colonial pig-headedness and the startling xenophobia of ignorance. But by the coming of the 'sixties the epithets of the 'thirties had fallen into discard, and indigenous Australians everywhere were the first to admit the new savours added to their lives as the result of "Continental influence." And they knew that without the huge, deliberate assimilation they could never have pushed ahead into new dimensions of progress.

WE HAVE NOT COME anywhere near far enough. We have learned to live in this challenging land of ours, and we have come to be a people who live enviably well with one another. In a land where nature is anarchical we have avoided anarchy and built a decent and healthy nation which could be a new Canaan for a harsher world. Yet the achievement, I think, is incomplete. Many of us are still in old fetters, an isolated and insular people possessive of what we have won but still uninstructed, often, in ways of living with other people . . . .

Here and there in eastern Australia one can still stumble across walls which the convicts built, of bluish granite or a mellow sandstone, now crumbling, choked or embriared in bracken and bramble. They were great builders, the convicts, of walls and fences, the work forced upon them. But after the convicts were free the people went on building walls and fences, and it became more than a habit and today in this continent of illimitable space we are still the greatest builders of protective walls and fences. It is almost as if there is bound to be something suspect or inimical in any intrusion from without.

Some of us seem to build our little palisades as guarantee that nothing *does* exist outside. To me, the most important lesson we, the friendliest of people really, have to learn is living with and understanding people who are quite different from us. A long time back we all had to learn to get on with each other . . . .

My grandmother was orphaned when her Irish father was drowned in a paddle steamer lost with all hands in the Tasman Sea while freighting mining machinery to Otago. She settled, in time, at Eaglehawk, near Sandhurst (before it was renamed Bendigo, after an English bare-knuckle pugilist), and lived in a tent town where she was befriended by Chinese diggers, and later met my Scottish grandfather who was partner with a German in a gold mine.

She was a gregarious and tolerant woman who loved the colour of people and the vibrancy of their

Penitentiary ruins, Port Arthur, Tasmania.

struggles in this gold-mad human antheap that covered more than a hundred square miles. At the turn of the century she and her own children were still close friends with two Chinese who had been born in the gold rush tents – she having midwifed one of them – and had struck up another friendship with a 21-year-old Russian Jew named Simcha Baevski, who had arrived in Australia only the year before and had become an itinerant peddler trudging the clay cart tracks with a prodigious pack of silks and small wares on his back. One of the Chinese became a barrister of repute, the other made a fortune as a vendor of herbal remedies, and the sweet-faced young Russian Jew Anglicised his name to Sidney Myer and established what would become the largest and most prosperous department store on the southern half of the globe . . . .

Any Australian of the third generation or more must be rather like this, going back like a rope

---

LEFT) Chinese burial shrine, Cooktown, northern Queensland.
RIGHT) Gold rush survivor, Hill End, New South Wales.

unstranding and fraying out into loose ends, and some of the ends almost always lie in the quartz and sand and grits of the early goldfields . . . .

They knew of the existence of gold in the government days, when English soldiers policed the severe land. But for years they kept it secret, fearful that colonial life would degenerate into chaos and authority would have its throat slit.

So it became more respectable to admire serene and formal pageantries than to recall, as my grandmother, those wilder days. And we have all of us been affected by this need to conceal an uninhibited youth. By the time I was growing up I had forgotten the kindliness of those Oriental faces my grandmother showed me in Bendigo, and the gifts of ginger in keepsake jars of earthenware. I read Sax Rohmer and watched Warner Oland's travesties of Fu Manchu, and on my way to night classes in Melbourne skirted with fear and revulsion the evilly smelling and dimly lit dives and dens – so harmless, really – of Little Bourke's "Chinatown." And that on the very same street where Sidney Myer worked late to extend his great department store . . . .

Somewhere along the line we cast off so many of the rich raiments of our yesterdays, and only recently have

LEFT AND RIGHT) One Hundred and Fiftieth Birthday pageantry, Bathurst, New South Wales.

we set out to find them again, and begun to shed old chauvinisms . . . .

The frayed-out rope is everywhere. In the little Tyrolean village of Telfs, at a *Gasthof* under the summit of Hohe Munde, a mustachioed mountaineer in leather breeches laboriously penned a letter for us to take out to an uncle who had gone out to South Australia when he was a boy. On the Moselle, in a little inn at Alf, there were tiny fires burning under all the pruned vines running up the slope to thwart the frost and the whole hillside was sparkling. We stayed up very late drinking white wine and watching the fires and the flow of the boats down the river on their way to the Rhine. The inn-keeper told us that the cuttings from his vines had been sent out to South Australia nearly a hundred years before, and he asked eagerly but graciously after the health of those transplanted vines, wondering about their fruitfulness and far-away harvests, and whether the moselle "out there" was also good to drink. It was a time of pause between

LEFT AND RIGHT) German festival, Hahndorf, South Australia.

German winter and German spring.

"Out there," we told him, it was now the time of harvest and of vintage festivals; there would be young men in *lederhosen* and girls in their dirndls, singing the songs of the Moselle and the Rhine and the Silesian fields. "Out there your vines have flourished," we told him.

And short hours before dawn he lit us to our bed, musing on the ancient magic of wine renewing itself, even so far away . . . .

We are not, as the phrase used to go in the old pharmaceutical instructions, the mixture as before.

RIGHT) Vintage Festival, Barossa Valley, South Australia.
FAR RIGHT) Yugoslavian church picnic, near Adelaide, South Australia.

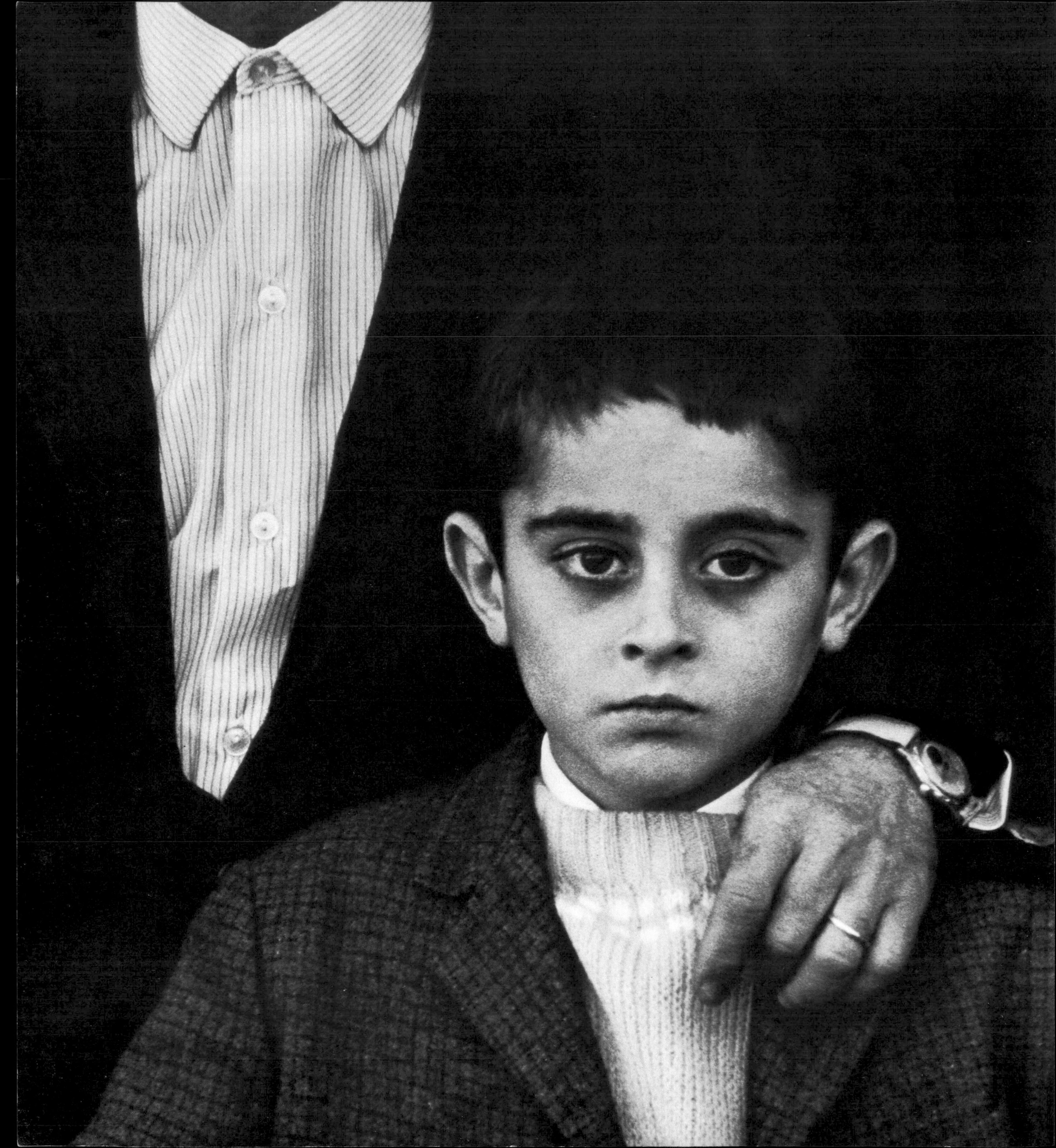

Nor are we solely involved, as some people suggest, with a choice between relinquishing an old and weakening British tradition and forging stronger links with an American one. As a people we are tied to many motherlands and enmeshed in a variety of old nostalgias. Yet for the young of whatever source and parentage, there will come to be only one motherland and that will be Australia . . . .

In Greece's Dodecanese Islands the departing emigrant takes a pebble with him from the shore and, as he looks back for the last time on the receding familiarities of his native soil, drops the stone into the

LEFT) Greek immigrants, Sydney.
RIGHT) British flag in honour of Royal Visit, Town Hall, Sydney.

sea to signify that he will nevermore return. It is a symbolic cutting of all terrestrial ties with home. Yet how much there is of his birthplace that he brings with him, how much in his heart that will go on aching and yearning for the established certainties and old assurances that he left behind.

It is said that the two most tremendous experiences of anyone's life are being born and dying. The third must surely be the sharp and anxious moment of a total commitment to a new life in a remote and alien country.

We cannot expect them – lonely and uneasy, needing time and friendliness

RIGHT) Immigrant arrivals, Sydney Harbour.

and understanding – to turn into Australians overnight. Nor should we want them to: our particular way of life is complex, not at all easy for any stranger to grasp.

What is needed, and what is now happening, is for us to learn also from them. Our own sometimes harsh outlines can be softened and refined by sympathetic absorption of other multicoloured and memorable pasts. Memory is the vital agent which helps us explore and define new worlds – their memories as well as ours.

Every generation is only a part of several generations; the one of now, the one of before, and the one to grow and thrive, all existing together, and all for a time needing each other. We should ask them, I think, to bring their pebbles with them . . . .

One summer evening in the Sydney suburb of Paddington I dropped in at a little Italian delicatessen. In the

LEFT) Mother and son reunited, dockside, Sydney.
RIGHT) Grandfather and Australian-born grandson, dockside, Sydney.

cluttered and redolent shop there were cloves of garlic drying, bottles of Lachryma Christi on the shelf, a tinselled Madonna above the till, and the smell of good pizza cooking.

At the rear of the shop, two steps and an opened door disclosed a heavily furnished sitting room where, at a table covered with faded green curtain rep, three children sat reading their English lessons. Behind the children, as if in some Neapolitan or Calabrian tableau, stood the adults, two men and three women, rigid and attentive to a ritual of wonderful mysteries beyond their respectful understanding, and their eyes were filled with all the hope and promise of the world.

One of the children, groping to explain the meaning of a particular word – I still remember the word, "suggest" – stared directly at me, but never saw me. Her eyes were focused beyond me, and far beyond the dusky outside, upon a world we have not even come to yet.

People bestow grace upon each other in curious and unexpected ways. We are no longer what we were, nor even what we are: we have taken the irrevocable step and we are already on the way to what we are to be. The painted signs, the hanging flags, all are of infinitely less importance than that pondering far-away quest that broods in a child's eyes. Perhaps she will discover enlightenment where we

LEFT) Yugoslav-Australian family at country picnic, near Silver Lake, South Australia.
RIGHT) Scottish competitor, St Andrew's Day Highland Dances, Adelaide, South Australia.

can at best find only dubious reassurance . . . .

James Cassius Williamson and his wife Maggie Moore came in 1874 from America to play the leads in the play *Struck Oil*, which they had picked up from a Californian miner. They stayed on and contributed a force to the Australian theatre which was to see out three generations. I have often wondered whether they could have dreamed of the juggernaut of hot dogs and ice-cream, hamburgers and barbecues, Coca-Cola and Levis, disc-jockeys and TV commercials which would someday follow them . . . .

Subtly, perhaps even a little furtively, we have crossed a line of no return.

LEFT) Meat pie vendor, Rockhampton, Queensland.
RIGHT) Australian "cowboys," Warwick Rodeo, Warwick, Queensland.
FAR RIGHT) American Indian teepee, by roadside, southern Queensland.

Last year the most sophisticated of young Sydney housewives were buying crocheted tablecloths from which to make smart cocktail dresses. Oriental restaurants were spreading into the suburbs. One of the season's most photographed weddings involved a third-generation Chinese nightclub proprietor and a wealthy, extremely beautiful third-generation Chinese girl (with two gorgeous fourth-generation Chinese children as attendants). Among my son's friends at high school were a Chinese boy from Singapore and a cultured Russian-Chinese boy born in Harbin. Everywhere I went I seemed to run into Asian students. We have crossed a line.

A Sydney technical college is now setting up a new kind of language laboratory, one vital object of which is to help Asian students to understand the deeper currents that move beneath the idiom of a people. As a scholar connected with this laboratory said, "We cannot expect an Asian to understand us simply by knowing a vocabulary and a syntax: he must develop a feeling, too, for Shakespeare and Alfred Deakin." As we, on our part, might consider developing a feeling for Li Po and Sun Yat-sen.

Still, we have made another in a series of beginnings. We have set our feet on a new path and, in time, our tread will grow firmer.

LEFT) Thai Colombo Plan graduate student in economics, Australian National University, Canberra, Australian Capital Territory.

The Land Builders

Most Australians would have been too preoccupied during the winter of 1950 to pay much attention to an adventure of immense significance which was beginning on their Great Dividing Range. Australian involvement in Korea that year was growing, a long run of government by Labor had just come to an end, people were tearing up rationing books and cards even though commodity markets were still a shambles and Black Market practices and practitioners hard to shake off. The Bomb and Cold War were disturbingly in everybody's thoughts, each city had a housing shortage problem that seemed insoluble, taxi drivers had grown rapacious, there were strikes everywhere. Some Australians were even saying, "Why don't we give this bloody country back to the boongs?"

But, as always, it was the best of times as well as the worst of times. In the lonely, lovely snow country of Australia's rooftop, not far from Kosciusko in that wild rangeland near the border between New South Wales and Victoria, an unusual body of men were beginning an adventure that would set the model for a new nation. In such a flat land the blue beauty of Kosciusko, 7,314 feet at its summit, towers. If it is no daunting Kanchenjunga, it was still the home of uplands horsemen and stockriders in an earlier romantic time, and source of the country's beloved ballad, *The Man From Snowy River*. It sits in a land still ringing, even after giant tractors and bulldozers have irreverently moved in, with the rattle of hoofs against the scree, and a melody of memorable place-names, Adaminaby and Jindabyne, Kiandra and Tumbarumba, Tumut and Tooma and Thredbo and Cabramurra. The new undertaking, officially the Snowy Mountains Hydroelectric Scheme, which had received Canberra's authorisation the year before, was the biggest engineering project ever in Australia, and one of the biggest of its kind undertaken anywhere. It was symbolic of the awakening era into which Australia was entering. The concept stood as bridge and link between the leisurely time past, the urgent now, and the potent future. It was, simply, a concept of vision, not of mere expediency, and as such set a new pattern of Australian development.

In total, the project would involve constant work for a quarter of a century and an expenditure of some $800 million of public money; it would cover an area of 2,500 square miles. Four rivers would be twisted from their courses and turned in new directions. More than 100 miles of huge tunnels would be drilled through the rocky hearts of mountains. Seventeen large dams would be built, including Eucumbene, currently Australia's mightiest. Nine huge power stations would be built, and more than 80 miles of aqueducts. The fruit of all this, in another generation, would be a great gridwork of 4,000,000 kilowatts of cheap peak-load power, flood and erosion control, and the regulated use each year of two million acre-feet of irrigation water for a thousand square miles of properties under irrigation.

The concept, in its magnitude and human audacity, is Australia's Great Wall of China, but built to peaceful ends, without the forcing of labour or fears of the barbarian coming. Its significance, direct and exemplary, for the Australian future is immense.

By the winter of 1951, when the snow-cats and snow-ploughs were pollen-yellow against the drifts of icy white, the faces of all Europe could be seen at night through the smoky lamplight in the improvised, gale-shuddered mess huts. For the Snowy Mountains Scheme was the first big application of new methods of attack and a new type of work force.

From the beginning, in this first of the great new assaults on earlier frontiers there were men on the Snowy from 28 lands. They had been sent by Australian scouts and recruiters abroad – construction workers and engineers and surveyors, lured to swell Australia's own labour force for the urgent post-war requirements of industry, housing, reconstruction and rehabilitation. Predominantly they were Europeans, from almost every country. There were men, too, from the U.S.A. and Canada, Western Russia and Siberia – lands of the big dams – and from East Africa and South America. In one of the cookhouses a Cambridge graduate in a soiled chef's hat made flapjacks and scalding coffee for frost-rimed men in mackinaws, while declaiming Sophocles' *Electra* in Ancient Greek. And there were some in that reverberating weather-board shanty who could follow him.

Until that first winter on the Snowy the Australians had seen – and often tried to tackle – the stupendous dimensions of their problem with their land. But they had never quite envisaged themselves as grappling with it on a scale commensurately stupendous, never committed the resources equal to the task. It was on the Snowy in the 1950s that the Australians found the twentieth century measure of themselves.

The Australian had entered the crisis years of war in 1939 as a particular person moving in from a particular landscape that is stark and austere yet familiar, like a Drysdale painting. He had come to know his adversary, the timeless grudging land, and, in his isolation and with the tools and heart he had, made his limiting peace with it, as the aborigine had before him. But the war tore away the barriers of distance and isolation, as the two decades since have outstripped sound and moved into space.

Although some were slow to realise it, Australia was suddenly a different picture from the time of the first peopling of the empty land – and unimaginable then. The humpy or homestead was no longer put together by a man squinting out the sight, and squaring his shoulders and getting down to tackling the hard timber with axe and calloused hands. Suddenly it was a time when plans were drawn in air-conditioned offices in coastal cities by men in suits of executive grey, and buildings prefabricated and freighted to distant sites. Development of the land moved more and more into the hands of big groups, of corporations and syndicates, of great companies, of investment banks, of huge governmental projects planned for posterity. In place of the old hand tools and animal transport, of individuals struggling separately for survival, there emerged a calculated strategy that is the sum of the beach-heads' strengths in resources, skills, sciences, capital, machinery, materials, manpower. It is from the beachheads that Australia is making the next leap forward, and the Second World War – the war of planned objectives and massive assault – was the tutor of these things.

It is the man in the executive suit who most often now is the frontiersman, thinking statistically rather than romantically, working on aerial survey maps rather than in sunbaked landscapes, using his muscles for squash and golf and not for handling steers in the branding yard or rams at the dip. In a land where a handful of men once ruled empires of grass, he still has to think big because the operation is big. He may be more materialistic and less picturesque than the earlier frontiersman, but everywhere across the continent he is beginning to prevail at a tempo undreamed of by his predecessors. Only he can now attack the prime objective, increasing the productivity of the land. Only through the *collective* energy of modern Australia can new victories now be achieved.

They will be achieved in two different ways. The first is by improvement and extension of the rural areas for stock or crops, by winning from the wilderness additional millions of acres for agriculture. The second is through a vast expansion of mineral prospecting and development. In both areas remarkable gains have been and are being made.

On the south coast of Western Australia, the Esperance country is the final outcropping of ancient Yilgarn, the oldest exposed section of the continent, once a desolate plain of white sandy soil blowing in the wind, an intimidating wasteland of swamp, dunes and stunted vegetation. In the Esperance Basin more than two million acres are now being converted to lush sheep and cattle country, simply by putting back into the time-impoverished soil its lost minerals – minute "trace elements" of zinc and copper mixed in with the superphosphate and sown down with clover for pasture. Within a mere five years this desolate landscape, where nothing had happened since the Kalgoorlie gold rushes, has been transformed into one of Australia's most prosperous, thriving and effervescent farming communities.

Three thousand miles north-east from Esperance, metamorphosis is coming to another wilderness, the 20 million acres of tangled brigalow scrub country, running south from central Queensland to the New South Wales border. Now, with government backing, Australians are scrub-clearing the brigalow with giant crawler-tractors and drag-chains, systematically burning it off and re-seeding it by air with such scientifically developed pasture grasses as Rhoades and Buffel and Green Panic. The despised and hopeless brigalow belt is turning into new and rich cattle-fattening lands, and attracting new settlers from all over the continent to what was once a settler's nightmare.

In a land of meagre or wayward rainfall, of rivers few in number and temperamental in character, the utilisation of water resources is everywhere a vital factor in building land-productivity. Ironically, nowhere is the problem more critical than in Australia's tropical north, which comprises one-third of the great brown continent. In the north, the battle to harness these water resources for the land has been joined at the Ord River. Presently the Ord Scheme supplies irrigation for only nineteen farms totalling 23,000 acres, the merest pinpoint in the millions of acres of the great cattle runs Ivanhoe and Argyle Downs, that everywhere surround it. But even this minimal control of the previously wasted waters of the Ord has proved a significant point: under irrigation splendid rice and cotton crops are flourishing; sugar will grow there, so will corn and fodder crops. This remote area can maintain a successful white tropical agriculture. The next planned step is the construction of a much larger dam and expansion of the area under irrigation, primarily for cotton, by an additional 120,000 acres. Coming are tropical legumes to provide dry-season fodder for cattle, and new methods of control and conservation of wet-season rainfall. In the quickening tempos of Australian development, it would be a rash man who would now predict the future of the Far North or its ultimate productive potential.

The land's recent mineral development tells a still more startling story and suggests even more challenging prospects. In the post-war years the use of aircraft and aerial mapping, with new methods of geological exploration, plus millions of dollars of gambled private capital, have all resulted in an entirely new picture of the resources of continental Australia. Old wastes regarded as hopeless for agriculture, too difficult or too remote for cattle, impossible country for the sustenance of human aspirations now turn out to be fabulously rich in a great variety of mineral wealth. Sometimes they are deeply embedded, sometimes just beneath the wrinkled skin of the sunburnt land. These discoveries are bringing many economic experts to believe that within the present generation mineral products may supplant wool as the major source of Australia's export revenue.

This new sort of "rush" in pursuit of mineral wealth began with a search for radioactive materials in a world moving into the atomic age. Prospectors found rich deposits of uranium at Rum Jungle in 1949, and more later near the South Alligator River and in the old workings of Radium Hill and at Mary Kathleen. The other intense exploration and search has been for oil. Australia had been looking for oil since the first futile well was sunk at Coorong, New South Wales, in 1892. In the last decade, subsidised by government funds, the search has spread everywhere and intensified. The rigs are there on the margin of the Arafura tides, on the treeless shell-encrusted bleakness of Barrow Island, in the mountains of Papua and New Guinea, on a storm-swept floating platform off shore in Bass Strait, on the inhospitable north-west coast first raised by Dampier.

Except for a modest flow from the Moonie Fields in Queensland, the Australians have yet to find oil in substantial quantities; and the uranium of Radium Hill, Rum Jungle and Mary Kathleen has become one more surplus twentieth century commodity. But the north-west, which so repelled Dampier three centuries ago, is now revealed as a land incalculably rich in iron ore, coal and other minerals. And the low red cliffs on the Gulf of Carpentaria, which Matthew Flinders noted in his journals in 1802 during his first circumnavigation of Australia, are the visible outer edge of one immense field of high-grade bauxite, estimated to contain 2,000 million tons of future wealth.

Now Australians are everywhere looking anew at their land. Ore-fingered Lang Hancock, once a dingo hunter, found rich deposits of blue asbestos at Wittenoom Gorge in the lonely Hamersley Range country. In 1952, on a mineral survey flight in the Hamersleys, he came down through a wild gorge which had sheer walls of iron ore, and so discovered a field of 600 million tons of ore, one of the world's richest. At around the same time, in the burning ironstone hills to the south-east, leather-tough Stan Hilditch was out prospecting for manganese. But, like Hancock, he found instead iron ore, millions of tons of it at Mount Newman. Hancock and Hilditch became millionaires overnight, and another step was taken towards changing the face of Australia.

The new patterns are everywhere in Pre-Cambrian and Paleozoic areas once considered out of reach, where men tried and were driven out, or which, never having known the thud of an axe, succumb now to bulldozer blade and caterpillar tread. From the topmost tip of the Cape York Peninsula to the far corners of the colder south, through the bauxite fields of Arnhem Land to the mangroved tidal flats washed by the Timor Sea, from the glittering receding wastes of the Pilbara to the snug green harbours of Tasmania, everywhere the Australians are out building their land, assaulting it now with a new technology.

It began symbolically, on the ice-white drifts and the ridges of the Snowy, this new assault, and only 15 years ago. Now there are men from 44 different lands working on the tropics side of Capricorn. Now, in a scarlet haze of bauxite dust, the yellow bulldozers clank and charge along the low Carpentaria shore of Flinders' journals, where mysterious mounds of millions of seashells still stand, perhaps as relics of some ancient coloured people who came to the silent, stubborn, empty land ages ago.

A huge Nippon Yusen Kaisha ore-carrier is there now, down from Yokohama to fill her steel belly with the red riches, riding the slack pellucid tide. Several thousand miles away to the west, where the Indian Ocean laps the shores of Cockburn Sound, another Japanese ore-carrier filled to capacity with export-earning alumina, weighs anchor for the long trip home. New images, these, to be set in this detached, remote landscape that seems to stand outside time, yielding only slowly, stubbornly.

RIPPED, RAMMED, GORED, gouged, stripped, spiked, drilled and blasted, the old land is now under an attack that pales the term "development." The Ord, Weipa, the Snowy, the Isa, Cockatoo, King Bay, the Esperance, Barrow Island and Tom Price, these are all the names of places where revolution is occurring. The birds climb quickly into the sky and the kangaroo stops his nibbling to stare curiously at the yellow-painted monsters roaring and grunting past his peaceful home.

In a land where once there were two-and-a-half million horses there are only half a million horses left, and each year the numbers grow fewer. In place of animal transport and old hand tools, there are now bulldozers and giant crawler-tractors, power shovels and graders and mechanical posthole diggers and road trains and airplanes. And each of them is committed to changing the face of the old land and shaping it to man's new ambitions . . . .

I am among the privileged, and certainly among the minority, of my countrymen in having made, aside from lesser journeying and excursions, two full and detailed circumambulations of this continent. Each time I went not as a tourist but as an inquisitive writer, and I went by truck and lugger and charter plane and Boeing jet as well as afoot. These two long journeys were separated by exactly a quarter of a century, and that is about the span of time in which the revolution on our land has occurred. One can sum this up, I think, by saying that despite the violence of the attack, we are building the land now, and not merely trying to conquer it. We are building it with machines, yes, but still with men, and a new breed of men at that. For however much

RIGHT) Heavy earthmoving equipment, Snowy Mountains Hydroelectric Scheme, New South Wales.

technology advances, this is a land staked down finally and made gainful by human sweat and muscle . . . .

Last year I was at Mount Isa, in a parched Capricornian world of red desert and pallid stippled spinifex. Mount Isa is like a whole section of a prosperous industrial suburb clipped out and pasted down on a wilderness as raw and baleful as earth can show. The road cattle trains come in from the western plains and to the East there is a new railway to carry out the copper, lead, zinc and silver along rails laid out like a pair of thin steel rules through 500 miles of sun-cracked plains to the blue, reefed Townsville coast, where coconut palms against a tropical Pacific sky are the final fences of immensity.

That day at Mount Isa – it was 106 degrees in the shade – I saw a Finnish copper miner going to his sauna bath. That evening I saw the safari lines of workmen portering home their beer, and in one of the oldest pubs there was a broad hole through the wooden toilet door, where an impatient miner had punched his fist in admonition to some tardy occupant. For all its suburban and prosperous air, "the Isa" has a pungent smell of frontiers. So it was throughout the journey,

RIGHT) Iron ore railway construction, Dampier, Western Australia.

men and their spirit and machines in contention with the land. Everywhere there was the smell of the old frontiers under new attack . . . .

All this took me back to that long journey 25 years earlier, when they were just beginning to build the first of the great inland roads, from Alice Springs to Darwin, and Mount Isa was beyond the edge of nowhere, and about the only "foreigners" you ever ran across Outback were aborigines and a few Chinese and an occasional Malay in the pearl ports, and nothing very much was happening inside the big country. Nobody was particularly confident that anything *would* happen – or concerned that it wouldn't.

Along the Adelaide River they'd contrived a vegetable garden to feed the Darwin garrison and I atc luscious tomatoes sun-hot from the bush. I also heard a prophet in khaki shorts and corporal's stripes promise,

LEFT) Power shovel, iron ore mining, Cockatoo Island, Yampi Sound, Western Australia.

"this country up here will grow
anything under the sun if
only you give it water . . . ."

The last three or four generations all grew up with a sense of the vast hinterland that pervaded even the cities, and this was a fixed pattern of standard images like a lecturer's set of lantern slides used over and over again. Sheep, cattle, wheat, the virgin bush, the ring-barked trees, the sand-blown mallee and worked-out diggings that were the scattered litter and debris of man's passings.

FAR LEFT) Lake Eucumbene Dam and power station from the air, Snowy Mountains, New South Wales. LEFT) Irrigated orange grove from the air, Murrumbidgee Irrigation Area, New South Wales; oranges in packaging shed, Griffith, New South Wales.

There was not much thought of technology in this earthy land of sweat and hazard and improvisation. If no country town of any stature lacked its Mechanics Institute or School of Mines, these were mostly places where the town met to borrow books and draw raffles and stamp around in the Canadian Barn Dance.

But the people of this new generation are becoming masters of a gigantic working technology which could never have been imagined even when the century turned half-way. We have already come far since that anonymous army corporal grew a plump tomato in the red sand of the North. Now we have symposia of high-degreed experts who tell us that if we continue to

LEFT) Irrigated rice paddies from the air in afternoon sunlight, Coleambally, New South Wales.
RIGHT) Bulk wheat loading into Russian grain carrier, Fremantle, Western Australia.

progress as we have since 1950 we can grow enough food for 60 million people within the next twenty years, and by the end of the century, enough for 500 million . . . .

How many of us, I wonder, are aware of the privilege we have – to be stall-holders in clear view of the stage upon which is about to be enacted one of the greatest of all Transformation Scenes? The object of the spectacle is to transform a continent. The actors and stagehands,

LEFT) Cotton harvesting, Wee Waa, New South Wales.
BELOW) Grainfields from the air, Darling Downs, southern Queensland.

highly skilled men, these, are technicians, explorers, surveyors, geologists, nuclear physicists, engineers, chemists and all builders. They are already well on the way to creating an unprecedented Australia.

They will find oil for us and pipe natural gas across the land as we once, with an earlier audacity, piped water across the deserts to Kalgoorlie. They will use nuclear power to build harbours, to treat metallic ores in remote mining sites, and to draw fresh water from the surrounding oceans. They will find

LEFT) Applying rain-permeable oil compound, sand dune stabilisation test planting area, Sydney, New South Wales.
RIGHT) Technician planting eucalyptus tree, sand dune stabilisation field test, Sydney.

new riches and challenge rivers and rainfall and the dead sour lakes of the land. They will take the surging 36-foot tides of the Timor Sea in the great tidal basins of the distant West Kimberleys, and from them harness 50 times the electric power capacity of today's Australia. These are no more pipe dreams than the Snowy was during that first winter in the snow, or the promises of that corporal growing his tomatoes in days before the Snowy was imaginable. Technology is always striding ahead of our imaginations . . . .

North of Capricorn, on that later trip, I counted men from 44 different countries. Everywhere, threaded through the nasal slow taciturnity of Australian speech, there was a new obbligato of strange rich cadences; the accents were different but the substance of their talk was the same as the corporal's 25 years earlier, of

LEFT) Mineral survey team south of Mt Tom Price, Hamersley Ranges, Western Australia.
RIGHT) Geologist sampling Limonite iron ore, Hamersley Ranges.

building the land and making it fruitful.

In the Pilbara, in the cabin of a power shovel, there was a face, reddened now by ore dust, which had once looked out through the barbed wire at Auschwitz and had made the long journey by way of steppes and the Pripet Marshes, and there was still a number tattooed on the wrist of the hand shaking on the gearshift. They played *tavli* now at Darwin as well as fantan, and called it *trik-trak* on the Katherine; and at Wittenoom Gorge, by the blue asbestos mine, the Ukrainians favoured chess.

An American group from Hawaii was handling land development on the Esperance coast, Arizonans were growing cotton on the Ord, and in northern Queensland there

---

LEFT) Iron ore workings from the air, Cockatoo Island, Yampi Sound, Western Australia.
RIGHT) Coastal ore carrier loading Limonite, Cockatoo Island.

were Texans from the King Ranch running cattle.

On the oil rig at Moonie, there was a French-Canadian speaking broken English to his mates and French to his reveries. In a survey camp on the East Kimberleys plateau, amid the crimson buttes and mesas, a Greek cook watched the willy-willies writhing on the hot plain and to himself sang a gentle song about an Hellenic sunrise called *Ximeroni* and other melodies about donkeys, cypress trees and far-away neighbourhoods. There was good Chianti in the bars at Innisfail, and in a cattlemen's pub in the Dawson

LEFT) Offshore oil drilling crew, Bass Strait, Tasmania.
RIGHT) Offshore oil drilling rig from helicopter, Bass Strait.

country someone had nailed an English homburg and a battered bowler to the ant-eaten rafters among the sweat-stained slouch hats, autographed, of visiting stockmen.

It was almost as if the world had joined Australia for the building . . . .

We are still involved with the possession of our land, and so with the persistent anxieties it engenders – water, resources of power, the placement of people in space, and the long stark stretch of our lines of communication. The task of the new generation and the next is to build the land, not merely try, as we did, to conquer it. To enrich rather than to ravage or merely to endure. And given the new men and new methods, the new machines and new attitudes of mind, there is no reason why the Twentieth Century should not end in the final triumph of the human spirit, the proper fusion of a land and its people.

LEFT) Offshore oil driller.

The Economy

Australia, as Alan Moorehead has written, is a country where every man had to be his own Robinson Crusoe if he was to survive. Today's stable, prosperous economy and the affluent society of the Australian cities create the illusion, even to a good many Australians, that the country has been providentially blessed. Just as there is a whole generation of young Australians who cannot hope or even be expected to have a true understanding of the era of the Great Depression, there is half a nation today who, never really having looked at their own country beyond the bitumen, cannot appreciate what heart-breaking labours it has cost, what desperate experiments and trials-by-error, to impress an economic civilisation on to this inhospitable soil.

For most of its history Australia has been considered a primary producer, particularly of wool and, after this, of bounties of grain, meat and other foods. This emphasis is as it must be in a country of such great size and such small population, a country with more than sixteen millions of acres of wheatlands and a human population outnumbered twenty-to-one by its animals. Yet like Defoe's lonely castaway hero, the Australian has continued to change, adapt, devise and experiment to make the best of his circumstances. Australia's record flocks of sheep number 170 million, more than in any other country in the world, and it produces more and better quality wool than any other nation. Yet even as these totals have been swelling, Australians have been moving off the land and into the urban centres, shifting their livelihoods from under the clear Australian sky into factories and offices. Today, one-third of Australian workers are employed in factories and within the next ten years, when the work force will grow to five and a half million, at least half of them will be factory workers.

Wool, in its greasy state, or as processed wool, has long been the most lucrative of all the country's exports. Yet this signals no easy or spontaneous burgeoning of wealth from a benevolent environment. Sheep have had to be bred for the finest fleeces, yet also adapted to an environment of sparse rainfall, poor pastures, extremes of temperature and climate, and pests and diseases. The lineage of the Australian merinos, which make up about three-quarters of present flocks, through mixture and re-mixture includes Spanish merinos, French and German breeds, the South African fat-tail and the royal merinos from the flocks of King George III.

Of the sheep brought out in the First Fleet only one wretched beast survived the shattering impact of the colony and its pitiless environment. Not until tough, ambitious and far-sighted John Macarthur purchased some merino sheep brought in from South Africa in 1797 did the hard-pressed little colony set Australia off on the course of its economic destiny. Macarthur decided to breed specifically for wool. He took some samples of the early shearing back to England, and on the strength of them got himself a rich land grant outside Sydney plus some rams and a ewe from the King's royal flock at Kew. Macarthur failed to establish the aristocracy of landed gentry he so earnestly desired, but the first exported parcel of Australian wool, only 245 lb. of it, sold in England for the excellent price of 124 pence a pound in 1807. Within twenty years the new settlement was mounting a major challenge to the woolgrowers of German Saxony, who had dominated the trade since medieval days. By 1851, when gold had added an unexpected new dimension to the colonial potential, Australia was producing more and better wool than any country in the world. It has maintained this supremacy ever since, although individual Australian producers have seen their earnings roller-coaster from a miserable few pence a pound to a high of 606 pence per pound.

The years since World War II have been as dramatic and significant as any since Macarthur's pioneering of the industry. In the last two decades numbers of sheep and production of wool have almost doubled thanks to the elimination of the rabbit plague on the sheeplands, pasture improvement through subterranean clovers and fertilisers and the use of trace elements in previously mineral-deficient soil. Australian wool today challenges the new synthetics as it once challenged the woolgrowers of Saxony, and in the frenzied cacophony of the wool sales, buyers from all over the world – Japan (now Australia's biggest customer), Britain, Red China, the U.S.A., countries of the Common Market, the U.S.S.R., Poland, Czechoslovakia, Yugoslavia – vie vociferously for their share of a golden fleece that can be worth 800 million Australian dollars a year.

Wheat, too, has had a long tortured story since the early colonists planted their first six scraggy acres in 1788, and failed, and tried again. More than 1,000 varieties of wheat have been developed to overcome the hostilities of the old land. The Australian farmer had to pioneer also in the contrivance of strange machines to help him surmount obstacles of terrain and scale – strippers and harvesters, the stump jump plough, seed drills and the combine – in order to build an industry now worth nearly $500 million a year to the country.

The cattle industry developed along similar lines from similar hopeless beginnings – breeding and cross-breeding to develop the strains which could graze across the dry reaches some of which could not support more than one cow per square mile. Dryness and distance drove the Australians to new concepts of agricultural and marketing technologies; Victoria was the site of the development of the refrigeration process which would, by 1879, see the ship *Strathleven* sail from Sydney for London, carrying a cargo of refrigerated meat for markets where the price was four and five times that in Australia. The growth has continued until Australia now produces a million tons of beef per year, an increase of 40 per cent in the last decade alone, and the new technologies promise some economic benefit at last from the vast empty acres of the North.

Everywhere and constantly in primary production, problems had to be challenged and overcome. The scourge of prickly-bear was wiped out by importation of the busy moth *Cactoblastis*, the plague of cane-beetle in Queensland sugar fields countered by importation of a giant toad from South America. Australians have had to bore for artesian waters in the dry lands and build systems of beef roads and great cattle truck trains to overcome the stupendous empty distances of the Outback. They pioneered networks of domestic airlines rivalled in extent and usage only by the U.S.A., and with the best safety record in the world. They developed new techniques of utilising timber resources in a land of unique but sparsely scattered forests of difficult hardwoods, among them 500 different species of eucalypt, 600 of acacia, the lordly mountain ash that was the tallest of the world's hardwoods, and millions of acres of dwarfed mulga. For a long time Australians were foolish with their timber — it should never surprise anybody that they are the world's champion axemen – and were obliged to import all their paper and wood pulp and most of their softwood sawn timbers. Recently they have devised a way of making pulp, newsprint and fine quality paper out of hardwood (never done before), and cutting beautiful veneers out of native woods. A rich and vital secondary industry now exists where only a generation before there was none at all.

When Australia entered World War II she was clearly definable as a primary producer. Her meat, wheat and especially wool paid for the manufactured goods which had to be shipped to her. She supplied the raw wool; Britain shipped back the finished textiles. She had industries of a sort, but by and large these were home-oriented productions catering to particularly Australian living patterns; she was hardly an industrial power. She had ample resources of fuel – black coal, the world's biggest single deposit of brown coal – and rich ore deposits; but although she did produce high-grade iron and steel cheaper than anybody in the world, she was virtually without heavy industries.

The Second World War severely re-shaped this conventional economic template. As sea lanes were menaced and the manufacturing of their suppliers diverted to production for war, Australians suddenly became aware of their overdependence on the outside world – and the economy began to change. Before the war Australians had assembled but never made a motor-car: today in open competition Australian-made cars outsell all others in Australia.

The changes have continued at such a pace that today, two decades after the war's end, most of the old economic stereotypes are either untrue or overlaid with new truths. Manufacturing became the single largest employer of labour; in proportion to population, as many Australians are today employed in manufacturing as in the United States. Although three-quarters of Australia's export income still derives from rural production, the totals have so risen and been supplemented by manufactures that the pre-war breadbasket country has become the world's twelfth largest nation in terms of international trade. Although some 90 per cent of all the land utilised is still classified as "rough grazing," mining and the processing of minerals have doubled since the war ended.

Since the war, established companies have grown at unprecedented rates, and completely new industries have sprung up. BHP, titan of Australian companies, has spent more than $500 million on expansion over the past five years. The company, founded by boundary rider Charles Rasp in 1885 with fourteen shareholders and capital of $30,000, today has 22 subsidiary companies operating coal mines, iron ore quarries, shipyards, iron and steel works, rolling mills and furnaces, and extensive exploration for offshore oil and natural gas. They produce, among countless other things, five million tons of ingot steel a year, and employ 46,000 workers.

Aluminium is perhaps the perfect illustration of the new. In spite of the immense demand for this metal in World War II, no aluminium at all was produced in Australia until 1955, and even up until 1960 all the bauxite used to make this aluminium had to be imported. But in the Darling Range of Western Australia, on the Gove Peninsula in remote Arnhem Land, at Weipa just down from the northernmost tip of Cape York, Australia found on the very skin of its own rejected soil bauxite deposits huge enough to last for hundreds of years. By 1963 Australia was self-supporting in aluminium requirements and hundreds of millions of dollars of overseas and local capital were being invested in the new wealth. Today, only a brief decade after the first experiments at Bell Bay in Tasmania, Australia is capable of making its own aluminium and of exporting local bauxite and alumina overseas.

The war did two vitally important things for Australia. It forced upon the country the necessity for developing its factory, mining and industrial capacities, and it was the instructor in new methods of attack, massed assault, combined operations and the employment of the full weight of new skills and techniques.

Once the new patterns were accepted the revolution was under way. Mineral production was to be trebled, factory output to increase twelvefold. Overseas companies established themselves and capital began to flow into the country as never before. Since 1948 nearly $5,000 million net have poured into Australia, 55 per cent from the United Kingdom and 35 per cent from North America, primarily the U.S. More recently the American proportion of this has increased until U.S. investment in Australia now totals some $2,250 million. Australia supplies some 90 per cent of her investment capital, but the foreign capital is vital in the spearhead efforts where the risks – and excitements – are greatest.

Already in the West, American involvement is prodigious – some $750 million of planned investment in iron mining, land development, alumina refining, oil exploration, cattle raising, cotton growing, plus the U.S. Navy's $89 million VLF (Very Low Frequency) strategic communications centre on North-West Cape and the eleven-million-dollar space tracking station of the N.A.S.A. at Carnarvon. Now building are 600 miles of new standard-gauge railroad, seven new towns, and three new deep-water ports capable of handling huge ore-carriers.

In most of these undertakings Australians have an interest, in direct and indirect employment and as subsidiary companies in the investment of capital. And there can be no question about the economic stimulus they provide. But in a new world economy constantly growing more complex, Australia is still but a junior partner and conscious of the fact. New questions are being asked: will new economic influences from without damage or destroy inherent Australian qualities or dangerously impair national independence? Does the development of a world economy, with Australia a part of it, mean that this country will be continually at the mercy of a British decision to enter the European Common Market, or American import and tariff policies on beef and wool and sugar and butter? The new trends seem, to some, to be making a convention of security (which had never before seemed possible in such an inimical country); some see Australians moving towards an acceptance of this *dolce vita* under the Southern Cross as something pre-packaged, gift-wrapped, and loudly huckstered on the T.V. commercials. More and more, chance and challenge are matters for the great corporations, often head-quartered half a globe away, and adventure seems to be in the company balance sheet but no longer on the far horizon. By this view, it is impossible that the Australian should not be changing into a different sort of person. In the new scheme of things it is now sometimes difficult to imagine the fanatically individualistic figure of a John Macarthur or a Henry Lawson.

But if these are reasonable questions, other Australians see it as a triumph to have built out of a harsh land an economy prosperous and stable enough to attract the multi-millions of investment capital from a moneyed older world. And this reflects a conscious governmental decision to move ahead slowly enough to be "solid." If the economic centres of gravity have changed, most Australians believe they are merely part of other changes everywhere. If Australia's own outlook is altering towards a more material and technological concept of life, they see this, however sadly, as part and parcel of the new times.

In a land forced to import 130 million barrels of oil per year there are now, thanks in part to foreign capital, discoveries which give hope of whittling this major drain on Australia's foreign exchange. At the same time China, which has barely touched Australia's destiny since gold rush days, is suddenly Australia's largest customer for wheat. And the focal point of this foreign interest today is Western Australia, the traditionally neglected State of the Commonwealth. Using the airplane and the combined assaults as well as the individual audacities of men like Hancock and Hilditch, Australians find they have at a conservative estimate some 5,000 million long tons of good quality iron ore, among the largest reserves in the whole of the western world. In 1960 the Australian Government lifted its ban on the export of iron ore, and Japan, once an enemy, now a friend, is ready to take for the next twenty years the output of these immense new ore fields.

Japan in John Macarthur's time was sealed off from the world in a guarded feudalism, not even yet to be parodied by Gilbert and Sullivan. But Japan is now by far Australia's biggest customer for wool and the biggest buyer for Western Australia's iron ore, the existence of which Macarthur could never have suspected. Who could have predicted the huge Japanese ore-carriers, down to their marks with Western Australia's iron ore, outward bound from Dampier's grim coast?

NOT LONG AGO I REVISITED a city bar where in the old days the newspaper crowd and the artists and writers, and poets and actors used to get together to put their frustrations and despairs down among the ranked glasses. It had all changed. It was packed with businessmen, alert in their executive suits, most of them young. They stood on the marble floor shin-deep in a ground-growth of briefcases as thick and as brown as summer bracken. The place had been renamed the Explorers' Bar, and all around there were murals of Bass and Flinders and Cook and Leichhardt and Sturt and Oxley . . . .

I find it hard to put my finger on the point where most of our people committed themselves to offices and to machines instead of to the land. It seems not all that long ago when one looked twice, and speculatively, at the saw-toothed roof of a factory or saw "industry" in terms of black mines and foundries and even the corner bicycle repair shop, and almost everything that was manufactured seemed to come from overseas. Now the older times have a nostalgic innocence, like the jerky unreality of old cinema sequences. What has really changed, of course, is our *attitude* towards this country and what we do with it, and this change began with those who were young in the last war and was made firm by those who are still young now. This change was, in fact, a slow realisation that legends were no longer reliable substitution for realities.

It was only very recently that we began to free ourselves from these potent myths of ours. The ram was king and the golden fleece was within our coat of arms as well as wrapped around our solvency. The squatter, being "boss" or representing class, had only an uncomfortable place in our worker's pantheon, resented as baneful authority or potential enemy.

RIGHT) Changing saw blades, paper mill, Burnie, Tasmania.

Struggle, the more hopeless the better, was glorified, but not success. This has always been the great and basic difference between the Australian and the American. Enterprise, especially "big business" enterprise, was traditionally regarded as alien. Only labour was home-grown; and it was labour largely for the mines and plains and forests and the ultimate movement of the products of the land.

Since 1880 we have been among the most highly urbanised of the world's people, yet we lived, most of us, in a curious pastoral idyll,

RIGHT) Station hands and beef cattle, Brunette Downs, Northern Territory.

where the wool was grown, grain and carcasses shipped, and it was part of life's natural balance that other people should make things for us.

All this may seem unreal now, when we are a greatly changed people in a vastly altered land. Australian industry has now grown secondary and even tertiary levels on top of the old primary foundations. It would startle most of us to peruse a list of industries, flourishing now, which did not exist in 1939; to consider the

BELOW) Shearing shed, Muloorina Station, eastern edge of Lake Eyre, South Australia.
RIGHT) Sheep from the air, north-western New South Wales.

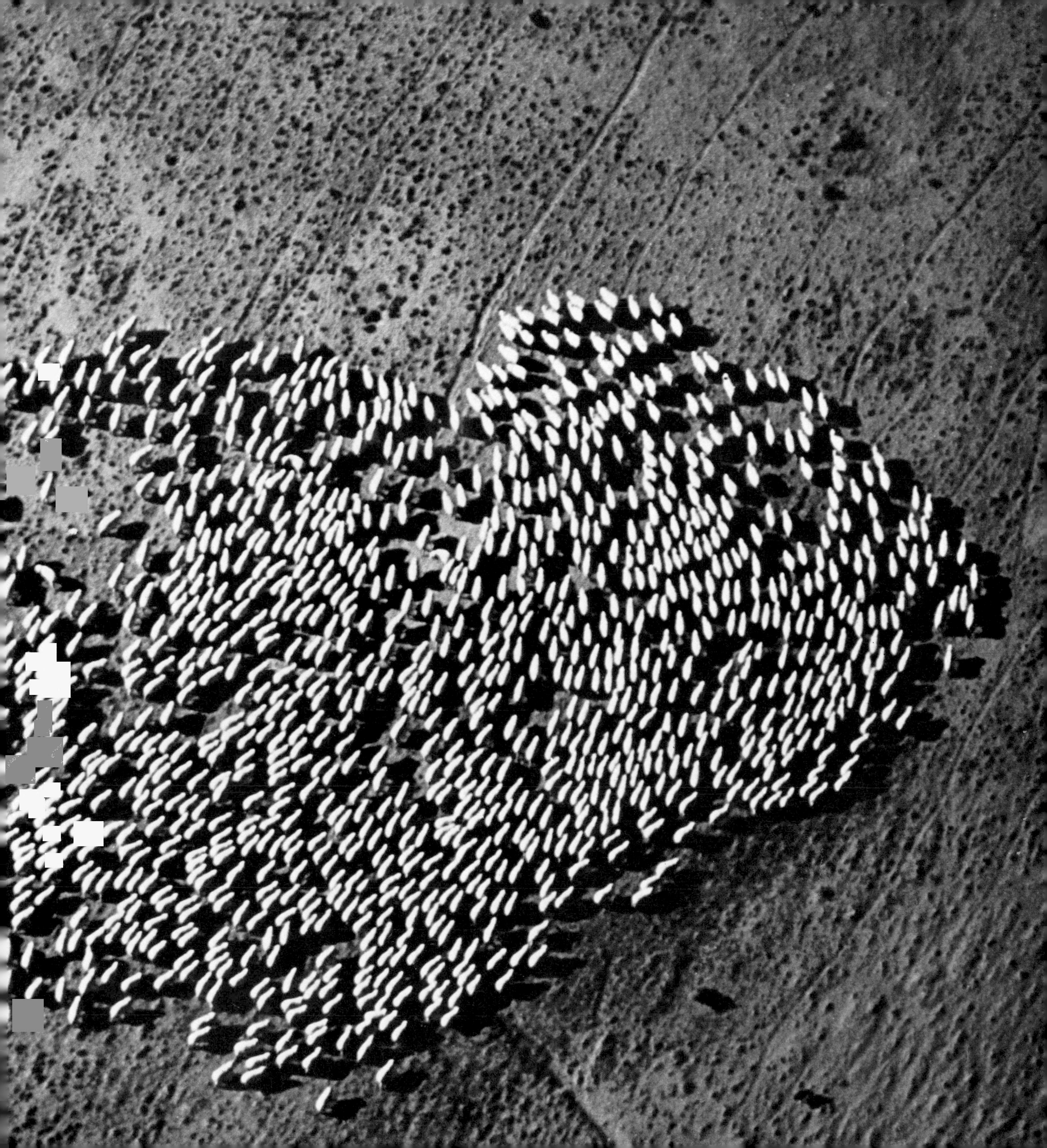

infinite range of goods made in this country which, so little time ago, had to be imported.

It is not easy clearly to chart the changes in a pattern when we are within the pattern and contributing to the changes and changing ourselves as well. But to come back after absence is to see the thing more distinctly, as one sees suddenly a child grown or a friend matured. When I came back to Australia after fourteen years, what struck me most about my countrymen's attitudes towards their livelihood was that some had begun to believe in success, and to be proud of achievement as well as struggle . . . .

Suddenly, with a new confidence, we were making our own things, both for ourselves and for others, spinning the fibres of tomorrow from the wool and the fibres of the trees, pressing out the pulps and essences and shapes into the new templates of boundless futures. Suddenly, we were importing the raw materials and machines, the chemicals and skills to help us make and do more in our own land. And we were sending away the price and surplus of our efforts.

And it was all being done not by turning our backs on the land and

LEFT) Mill worker through carpet loom, Melbourne, Victoria.

BELOW) Wool felt manufacturing, Sydney, New South Wales.

the primary wealth it offers us, but by raising new economic structures on the old primary foundations, the old engendering the new and growing stronger for the birth, and by discovering new wealth and opportunity beneath the skin of the old brown land.

It was remarkable and heartening to see these things in a country once thought dependent and suspicious of this kind of enterprise . . . .

And as I moved across Australia there was a parade of images, the brushstrokes in a mural of the new economic generation which had sprouted from the old.

I think of Kwinana and the new alumina refinery there, bitten out of western foreshores on the edge of

LEFT) Eucalypt timber for papermaking, Burnie, Tasmania.
RIGHT) Quality control sample, papermaking, Burnie.

the booming Indian Ocean surf. I think of Gladstone, where an iridescent sea runs clear to the Barrier Reef and the brolgas fly above, and of the smelter that has arisen on the sun-swept tip of Point Henry, in Victoria's Corio Bay.

I think of steel and Kembla, with the soft green Illawarra hills behind and purple mountains, and the winding road through Dapto to the lakes and Minnamurra and Jamberoo, and on the rolling rises the great tents of the Moreton Bay figs, the sentinel pagodas of the Norfolk Island pines, and the shaggy tufts of the cabbage palms – all this near and visible beyond the blasting glare of furnaces, the flood of molten metals, the slender pencils of the chimney stacks. And Newcastle, venerable among our industrial towns and named for black Tyneside, yet still fresh with sun and Pacific surf and a green-banked river running back to slopes of vines.

I think of a man in a mill in Townsville playing the control console of a machine with an organist's skill and dedication, building through the diapason of the hissing hammers a running,

BELOW) Aluminium ingots, alloying furnace, Point Henry, Victoria.
RIGHT) Steel making, Basic Oxygen System, Newcastle, New South Wales.

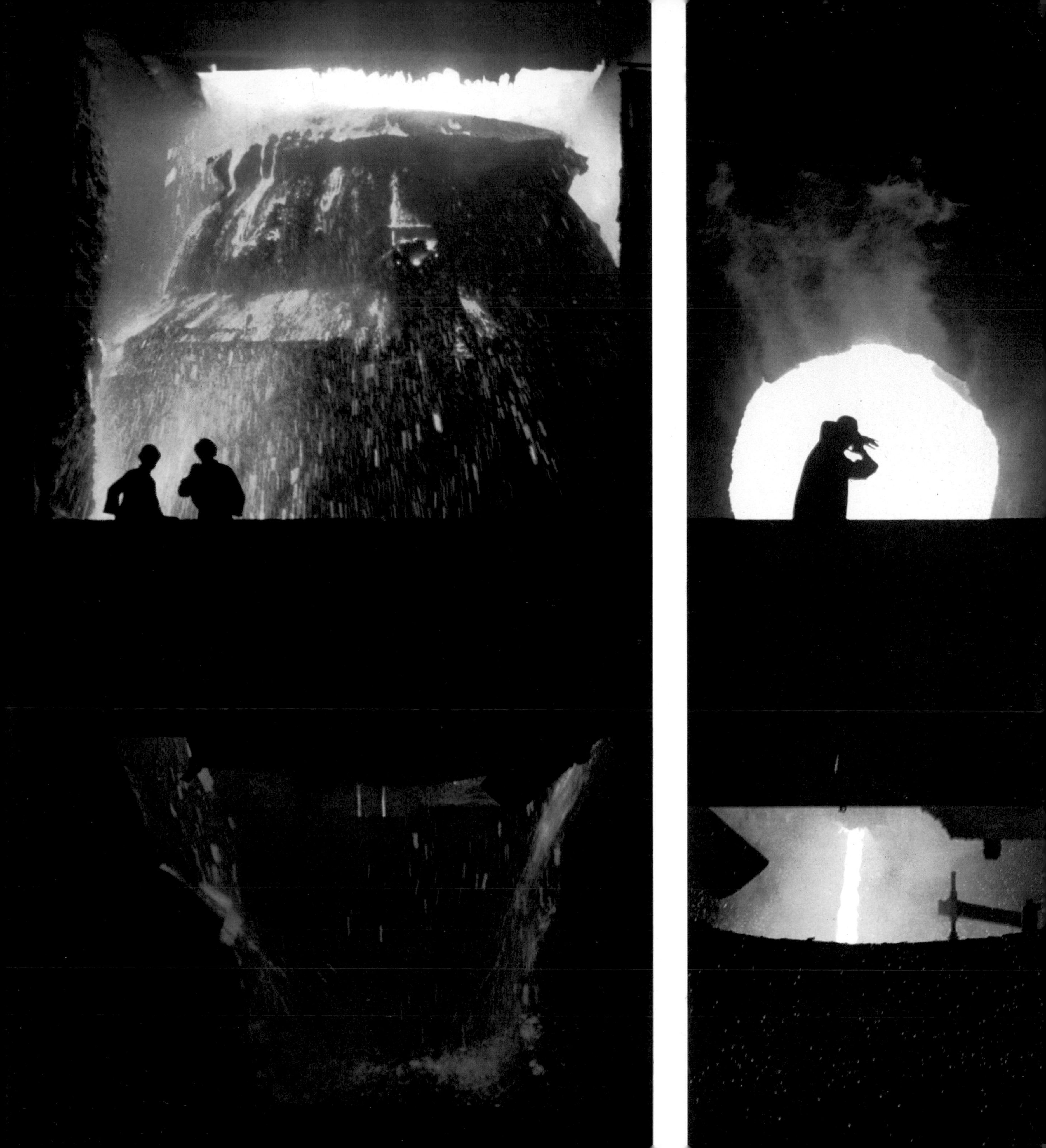

flouncing, writhing, whipping white-hot copper coiling into threads of ruddy wire, and the mill set in tropic trees hung with fruit bats on the edge of the Coral Sea . . . .

From the lone weathered battlers, risk-taking and response to challenge have shifted more and more to the province of the banker, investor, capitalist and industrialist. These men, once collectively maligned in the political cartoons of a working man's Utopia, have become the principal architects of our progress. It is almost as if they had taken inventory of us, their countrymen, and judged us as stable and on the whole thrifty, solvent and to an extent affluent even, and taken note of our pride in never having defected on what we owed. Since we have these good assets, and are a young people not yet weary or dispirited by lost illusions, we are therefore a good risk.

In our foreshortened world this has meant not a handful but a host of new allies. For the new architects are members of an international fraternity, travelling from continent to continent exchanging ideas and opportunities like seed-darts on the wind. And their membership in the fraternity has enabled Australia's

TOP RIGHT, LEFT TO RIGHT) Mr Bede B. Callaghan, Managing Director, Commonwealth Banking Corporation; Sir Ian Potter, Financier and Sharebroker, Ian Potter and Company.
BOTTOM RIGHT) Dr H. C. Coombs, Chairman of the Board and Governor Reserve Bank of Australia.
FAR RIGHT) Boeing 707 in Repair and Overhaul Section, Kingsford Smith Airport, Sydney.

integration with the world's economy, just as the men who forged our national systems of transport opened for us the day when our economy could become that of a nation rather than a collection of beachheads . . . .

Fortune has worked kindly for this country. We have grown industrial in an enlightened era, and so we have been saved the suffering gangrenes of an older industrial world. The mighty among our industrial colossi stand by surf-loud beaches and blue bays, the hearths and ovens and furnaces and stacks are swept by clean salty airs with sunlight dropped between.

I think of those black, dank, dripping streets I have walked in Lancashire and Yorkshire mill towns, and the hot hearth and furnace places of Illinois and Pennsylvania, and if we are to be an industrial people I count us blessed with a blue

---

LEFT) Truck assembly line, Dandenong, Victoria.
RIGHT) Loading wool for Japan, Fremantle, Western Australia.

五明丸
GOMEI MARU

sky still and a bluer sea at close hand,
and sunlight on the cottages and
people unstunted and undismayed,
and green, unblighted things
around . . . .

The realisation is clear and grows clearer as more of the ancient land mass is probed and scratched, that we must be served better by the new ways than we were by the old. The technical world of the immediate future will be one of gas and liquid fuels, new power sources including nuclear, still a world of steel, but of aluminium also and magnesium and metallic alloys, of glass and plastics and synthetic rubbers and ceramics.

On all these things we have made our beginnings and new intelligences and confidence are lending us impetus towards our future. With such new allies, and their companions in capital and the new technologies, we are moving out on the long road we must yet travel. Even nature, which we thought one-sided and ranged against us, is beginning to show another face when we care to look for it.

LEFT) Alumina refinery, Kwinana, Western Australia.

The Sciences

There is a common species of comfortable Australian who shuns erudition as "sissy." Specialised knowledge, unless of sporting statistics or employed for gain on TV quiz sessions, he considers useless if not embarrassing. This is another of those curious anomalies which beset so many facets of Australian life. For so much of Australia's early history – and so much of her future – is rooted in science. *Per capita*, Australia has always produced a remarkable number of original minds which have given much to their nation and some excellent benefactions to mankind, ranging from penicillin to straight bananas.

Everything began, in fact, in an atmosphere of scientific excitement. Cook's momentous voyage of discovery started largely as a scientific expedition sent to the South Seas in 1769 to make observations at Tahiti of a transit of Venus. His ship's company included outstanding scientists who were to be among Australia's earliest distinguished visitors; fittingly, the first point of landing was named Botany Bay, for the vast variety of new scientific specimens found there, and its two headlands, Cape Banks and Cape Solander, after the eminent English and Swedish naturalists who accompanied the expedition.

Permanent settlement hardly stilled the excitement. The platypus and kangaroo provoked wild controversy and admitted bewilderment among English naturalists, many of whom suspected that they were victims of a zoological practical joke. Steel-engravers had field days producing plates of the bizarre fauna of the new colony, and eager ornithologists began on the formidable task of classifying over 650 different species of Australian birds. At 27, Charles Darwin, himself to alter so much of his century's scientific thinking, came as official scientist on H.M.S. *Beagle*. Twenty-three years before publication of his famous *The Origin of Species*, he saw Sydney and Hobart Town, crossed the Blue Mountains and gathered much information about the Continental Shelf, and articulated his theories on the growth of coral reefs.

Australia's scientific heritage, therefore, is a sound one, well-based in the excitements and enthusiasms of adventurous new discoveries. The newly discovered continent's unique challenges added some special stimuli.

If the near-genius Lawrence Hargrave was himself too extraordinary a man to epitomise anything, his story is perhaps illustrative. Sixteen years old when he came from England to Australia in 1866, Hargrave failed to matriculate to Sydney University, and became instead an assistant to the astronomer at the Sydney Observatory. There he was a brilliant mathematician who discovered a number of stars. But there was also in Hargrave that deep, enigmatic compulsion that seems to drive certain Australians to audacious adventures on unlikely frontiers as a kind of compensation for disappointment on the more obvious boundaries of their physical environment. While still in his twenties Hargrave had pressed beyond these visible geographical frontiers – to the Gulf of Carpentaria, the Barrier Reef, Torres Strait, the Fly River in New Guinea – and had suffered many adventures, including shipwreck on the Reef and attack by aborigines in Queensland and head-hunting cannibals in New Guinea.

Back again in Sydney, working alone and generally ridiculed as a crank by his compatriots, Hargrave became an example of that kind of human oddity which Australia tends to produce in comparatively large numbers – a species of colonial maverick who, seeming to work outside his chosen field of endeavour, contributes deeply to its developments. In his suburban workshop Hargrave challenged the more abstract frontiers of theoretical science, painstakingly evolving interminable and strangely exact models of the movements of worms, snakes and birds, the currents of air and water. From all this he developed some visionary yet highly practical concepts of aerodynamics. He built models of aircraft, which flew, and in November of 1894, on a beach south of Sydney, succeeded in lifting himself sixteen feet into the air on four box-kites. He developed a rotary engine, and produced power-propelled model flying machines. In other circumstances, Hargrave might easily have anticipated by several years the Wright Brothers' first heavier-than-air flight. But Hargrave suffered the misfortune of being far ahead of his time in the colonies, too isolated by Australia's distance to benefit from the main currents of practical aviation development. Not until some 70 years later did he receive his nation's recognition.

A generation or so after Hargrave's experiments had seemingly been forgotten, a whole gallery of Australian aviators were, for no immediately explainable reason, pioneering the world's air routes. Ross Smith, Keith Smith, Parer, Mackintosh, Kingsford Smith, Ulm, Taylor, Hinkler. All the major oceans of the world were first flown by Australians with the single exception of the North Atlantic, and this ocean was almost notched in 1919 by the legendary Harry Hawker, a giant figure in British aviation who was born in an outlying suburb of Melbourne and left school at the age of twelve to dream of flying. These are all facts in the history of aviation, no less remarkable for their illogical origins.

But neither is it easy to explain why an Australian, Gordon Childe, should have become the world authority on the pre-history of man; or another

Australian, the late Sir Grafton (after the New South Wales town of his birth) Elliot Smith, a monolithic figure among anatomists and anthropologists; or why Sir Howard Florey of Adelaide, who would share a Nobel Prize for his work in 1945, should have been the man to discover in 1943 the means of extracting penicillin from the mould discovered by Fleming, and so saving countless human lives.

Yet this is a persistent Australian theme – an incorrigible capacity for audacious thinking. In spite of the relative paucity of Australia's population, this trait has enabled Australians to make important contributions to such widely diverse fields as radar, electronics, theoretical physics, biochemistry, radio-astronomy, virology and immunology, soil chemistry, micro-climatology, plant research.

One objective key to Australia's disproportionate scientific contribution has been the effectiveness of her research organisations. Two of these, the Commonwealth Scientific and Industrial Research Organisation, and the Walter and Eliza Hall Institute of Medical Research, grew up in Melbourne, almost side by side. A third, the Australian National University at Canberra whose research schools of physical sciences, medical research, social sciences and Pacific studies, have chalked up prodigious advances in these fields, was to see its own Sir John Eccles share a Nobel Prize in 1963 with Professors Hodgkin and Huxley for discoveries on the ionic mechanisms involved in the nerve cell membrane. The CSIRO, as it is known, has a present staff of more than 5,000, including 1,600 graduate scientists and is Australia's largest scientific body. CSIRO began only 40 years ago as a handful of people working in a group of rented rooms in the genteel decay of an inner Melbourne suburb. Near by and at about the same time, the Walter and Eliza Hall Institute was just getting on its feet. Initiated by funds from one of the first charitable trusts in Australia to be interested in science, the Institute began as an adjunct to the Melbourne Hospital. Except in terms of its achievement, it deliberately remained small, dedicated to the belief that the ideal system for co-operative research is defined as a small group of scientific workers involved in close personal discussion and engaged in no more than two major fields of inquiry at once.

International attention first focused on the little Institute in the 'thirties because of its work on the toxins and its startling work in virus research. From cultivation of the influenza virus in the chick embryo, discovery of the different strains of polio virus and identification of the "Q" fever virus, Sir Frank Macfarlane Burnet, a country boy from Victoria, gradually but deliberately moved the Institute into immunology and the theory of antibody production. In 1960, achievements in this field won for this remarkable medical scientist the Nobel Prize, and for the Institute acknowledged world leadership in its area of medical research.

Through clinical studies of gastroenterology, Burnet and his co-workers then moved into the virtually unexplored area of auto-immune disease and the mysterious functions of the thymus gland. The precise functions of the enigmatic thymus had never really been understood before Burnet and the Melbourne workers produced their startling evidence that it was a vital source of the body's immunities. In turn, this has led the investigators into the darker domains of auto-immune disease. The first textbook in this very new field, just published in the United States, was written by the Melbourne workers.

"We are concerned," Sir Macfarlane Burnet explains, "with cells which should protect the body against foreign invaders but mistake the nature of some cells of the body and attack them *as if* they were foreign." His little Melbourne Institute has contributed a brilliantly sustained body of original research to international medicine, and stands as another example of Australians overcoming isolation and remoteness from central sources, and attacking the far frontiers of the intellect in a land where the physical frontiers have still to be finally won.

Where it suited the Walter and Eliza Hall Institute to remain compact, the CSIRO has expanded enormously. Where the Walter and Eliza Hall Institute has probed the far intellectual frontiers, CSIRO's primary concern has been with making the best out of the Australian environment and resources. CSIRO's 32 major divisions reach from microcosm to macrocosm, from the world of the electron microscope to the rushing stars of outer-galactic space. It is concerned with plant research, soil chemistry, animal health, oceanography, fisheries, radio-astronomy, climate and meteorology, coal, mathematical statistics, physics, applied physics and radio-physics, pests and building materials, to name a few. In a country where the land itself remains the greatest challenge, it is not too much to say that there is no organisation which has paid off so well; nobody could even begin to calculate the millions of dollars CSIRO has added to or saved the national economy.

It is rather taken for granted now that Australia is one of the world's great primary producers, but, since the very beginning of settlement, Australian agriculture had to depend almost entirely on imported crops and pasture plants. They came from England, from Rio de Janeiro and Cape Town, from

Asia, the Mediterranean and the tropics. Some grew and a good many died in their strange new surroundings; some brought with them costly scourges for which the Australian environment had no natural enemies.

The five rabbits which came to Australia with the First Fleet were domesticated and seem to have behaved themselves, but the few wild rabbits given their freedom on a farm near Geelong in 1859 grew to a plague of such dimensions that the verminous race was estimated to number 1,000 million in Australia before the human population had reached three million. In 1887, only eight years after the first rabbit was reported in the colony of New South Wales, bounty-payments had to be met on 27 million scalps. Thousands of miles of rabbit-proof fences in southern Australia proved futile; the rabbits crossed the terrible Nullarbor Plain, penetrated one fence, got through a second fence hurriedly thrown up beyond it, and settled down to eat the country away. It was not until the 1950s that the CSIRO finally brought Australia's worst plague under control by introducing and spreading the myxomatosis virus and devising an effective use for the powerful poison sodium monofluoracetate 1080. Over the better part of a century rabbits had cost the country incalculable millions in erosion and stock losses.

Under the CSIRO and other government bodies the principle of cherishing the difficult Australian earth is working now to stricter scientific patterns. Some of the principal efforts, as is proper in the most arid of all continents, are concerned with climate and rainfall, evaporation and desalination. And of this work, some of the most original is being done in the CSIRO's Division of Meteorological Physics. There, Australian scientists are now intensively exploring what is called the "boundary layer" – the space of up to only 100 feet above the skin of the earth – which creates a startling 95 per cent of the earth's weather. Studying surface and sub-surface moisture evaporation and the transfer of moisture and solar energy in plant and animal life, Australia has achieved acknowledged world leadership in this new field of micro-climatology. Beyond research itself, Australian scientists have developed instruments for studying the climate of a microscopic world at the junction of air and earth, instruments which can measure the day's heat loss of a single blade of grass or the evaporation from a grain of sand. Somewhere here perhaps, as research continues, the Australian may yet find some of the secrets of making rain where he needs it and when he needs it.

Not all Australian scientific endeavours have been on this scale. Some years ago Australian geneticists managed to develop a banana which grew straight in shape, a development which promised not inconsiderable economies in packing. When Australian housewives steadfastly shunned the straight banana as unfamiliar, hence suspect, the banana research took a new turn. The same scientists are now perfecting a pineapple which grows square in shape, again promising substantial savings in processing and storage. Its fate in the market place is yet to be determined.

Australia's importance in space exploration has been a natural outgrowth of its pioneering work in radio astronomy. When America's Mariner-IV satellite moved into Mars's atmosphere, the first close-up photographs were transmitted via the Australian space-tracking station at Tidbinbilla, near Canberra. CSIRO has been responsible for much of this pioneering development, and the chief of its Division of Radiophysics, Dr E. G. Bowen, was one of the original groups of scientists in Britain who developed radar just before World War II. The huge steerable radio-telescope near Parkes, New South Wales – a gigantic, beautiful, lacy dish of 2,000 tons of steel mesh measuring 210 feet in diameter – was erected by the CSIRO in 1961. The Radio Heliograph under construction in pastoral country near Narrabri is also the brainchild of the CSIRO, while another radio telescope, the Mills Cross, near Canberra, is an innovation of the Sydney University's School of Physics.

These huge and curiously graceful metal structures, new and improbable silhouettes in the Australian landscape – "bloody funny gadgets to be stuck in a sheep paddock!" as a grazier said recently, scratching his head – are trying to get to grips with the riddle of cosmological beginnings, and the geographies not only of our galaxy, but of other galaxies remotely beyond.

Australia now has ears to this universal order and chaos – the clouds of astral dust and explosive gases, radiations and streams of cloud and orbiting planets and asteroids, meteor showers and cosmic rays and charged particles, neighbouring galaxies and the nebulae far beyond, white-hot blue stars and giant receding red stars, stars dying and stars being born – the whole frantic rushing whirling mystery of creation. To all this the steel dishes listen, reporting back through a scratching murmur that sounds like the static on a short-wave radio, to inky stylos, turning of reels of graph-paper, and the astrophysicist, who is a sixth-generation descendant of those men who sailed with Cook in the little barque *Endeavour* to make calculations of a transit of Venus. These radio emissions are the carefully hoarded evidence that one day may prove our cosmic origins. Strange things, as the grazier observed, to be occurring in an Australian sheep paddock.

THERE ARE TWO DISTINCT Australias, an old and a new, and for the time being they are living side by side, sometimes uneasily . . . .

Science is the one branch of our being which has survived the sea change unimpaired. Here one sees none of the jarring dislocations and discontinuities which have affected or are afflicting us elsewhere. It is about all we have still sacrosanct of an earlier tradition, of unwavering continuities preserved.

Yet within this orthodox framework of learning and research – where we have not broken with our tradition – the flame of our adventurous spirit burns most brightly. It is not merely that our scientists have avoided insularity by their own travels abroad, nor that a great many of them are not born here at all (for years to come we shall be hungry for scientists from other lands): it is, rather, that science exists and develops only by the universality of its respects.

There can be no such thing as purely Australian science, only an application that is uniquely or even consistently Australian. We cannot be pioneers, as we have been, in many of the fields of radio astronomy without a precedent of Galileo and Copernicus, of Tycho Brahe and Newton and Einstein – not dagoes and balts and poms and fritzes, but the giant explorers beyond the unnationalised frontiers of the mind. So in the cow paddocks, where the meshings of our huge metallic ears

RIGHT) Southern Hemisphere sky from the centre of the Parkes Radio Telescope, Parkes, New South Wales.

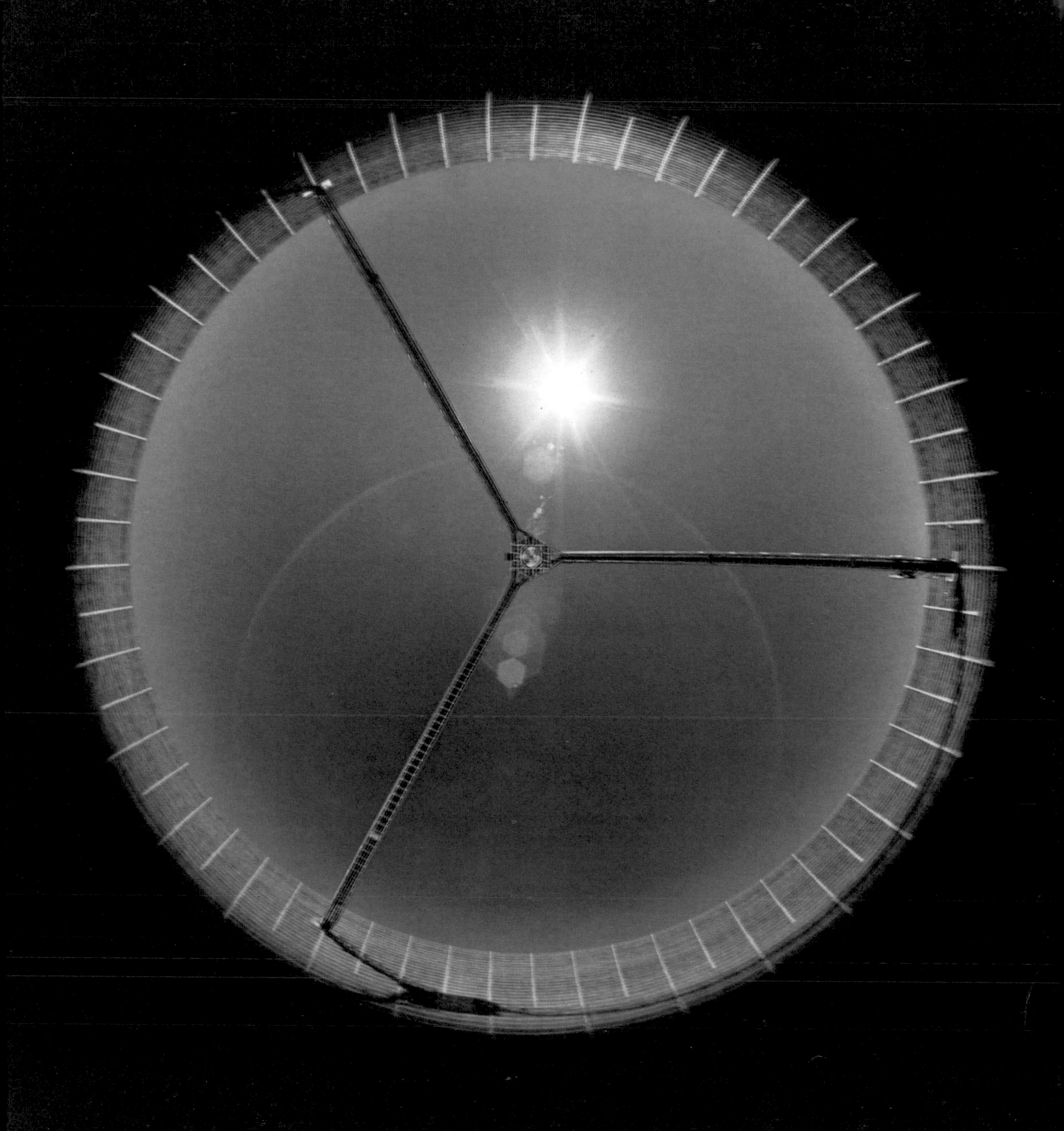

are cocked to a music of the spheres and mysteries of enigmatic quasars at the fringes of the universe, where a computer can devour a million separate messages in a night, where events which occurred before the dinosaurs left the earth have bearing on the inky squiggles of a stylo, where distant galaxies are studied through the scratchings and raspings and groanings of space – in such adventures as these we are one with a steadfast line of tradition, and in

LEFT) Parkes Radio Telescope at sunset.
BELOW) Radio astronomer monitors raw data from the Parkes Radio Telescope.

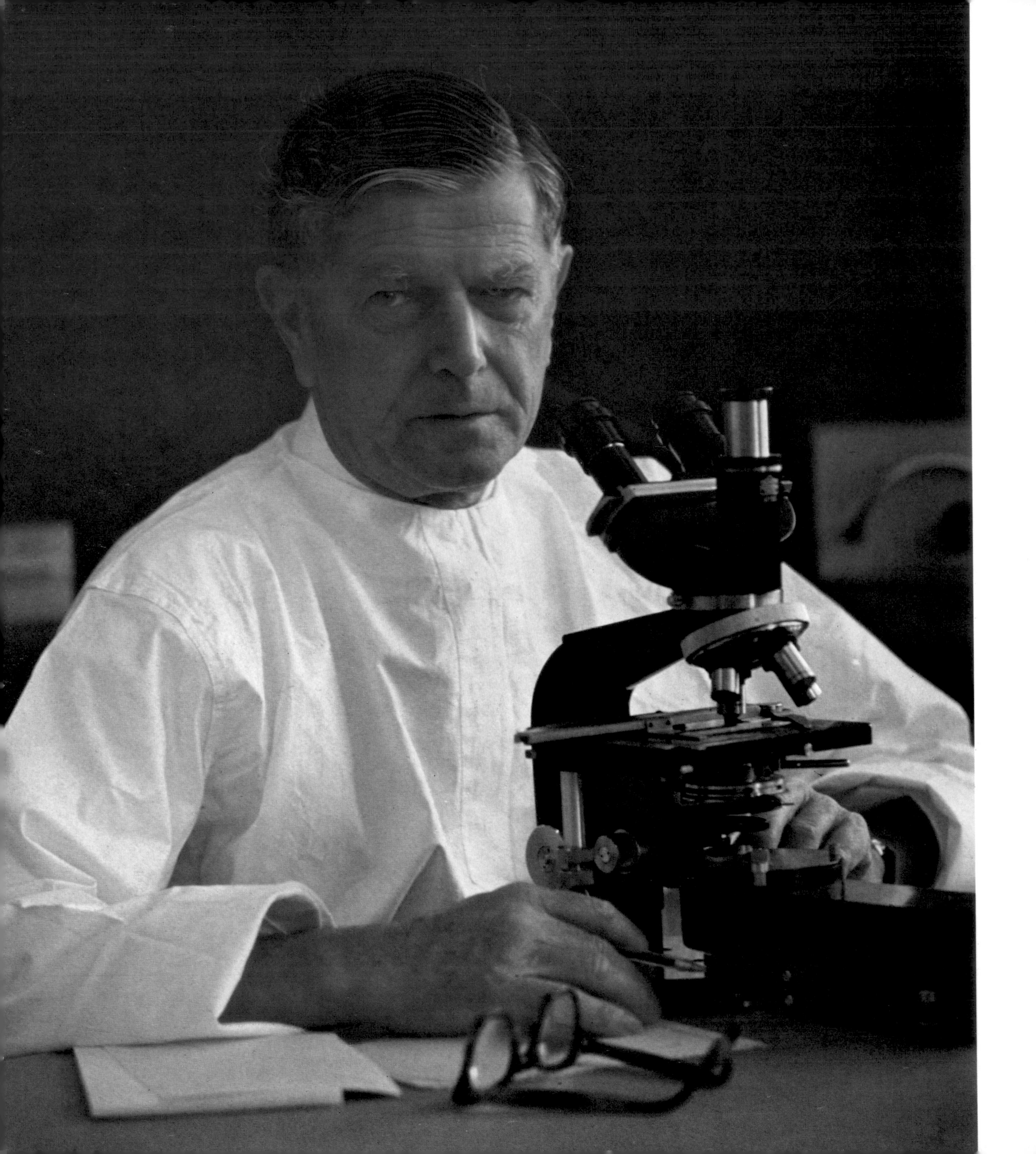

good and cosmopolitan company. There is no dead and empty desert at the heart of our science, and the prospects are infinite . . . .

Yet there is a robust, almost rollicking Australian quality about our science – our arts have this, too – which allies the best of our intelligence and ideas with an exuberant and almost old-fashioned zest for the game and the adventure and the challenge. A friend tells the story of being on a scientific expedition in the frozen wastes of one of our Antarctic dependencies – we keep scientists the year round in these far-away places. His group were with some difficulty making for a gigantic outcrop of black rock rising above the lonely landscape of frozen hummocks and crevasses. When they reached it they saw an Australian, like a later Amundsen, had preceded them, and in bold whitewashed letters on the rock had proclaimed: "Science gives me the trots . . . ."

With or without irreverence but always with gusto and dedication,

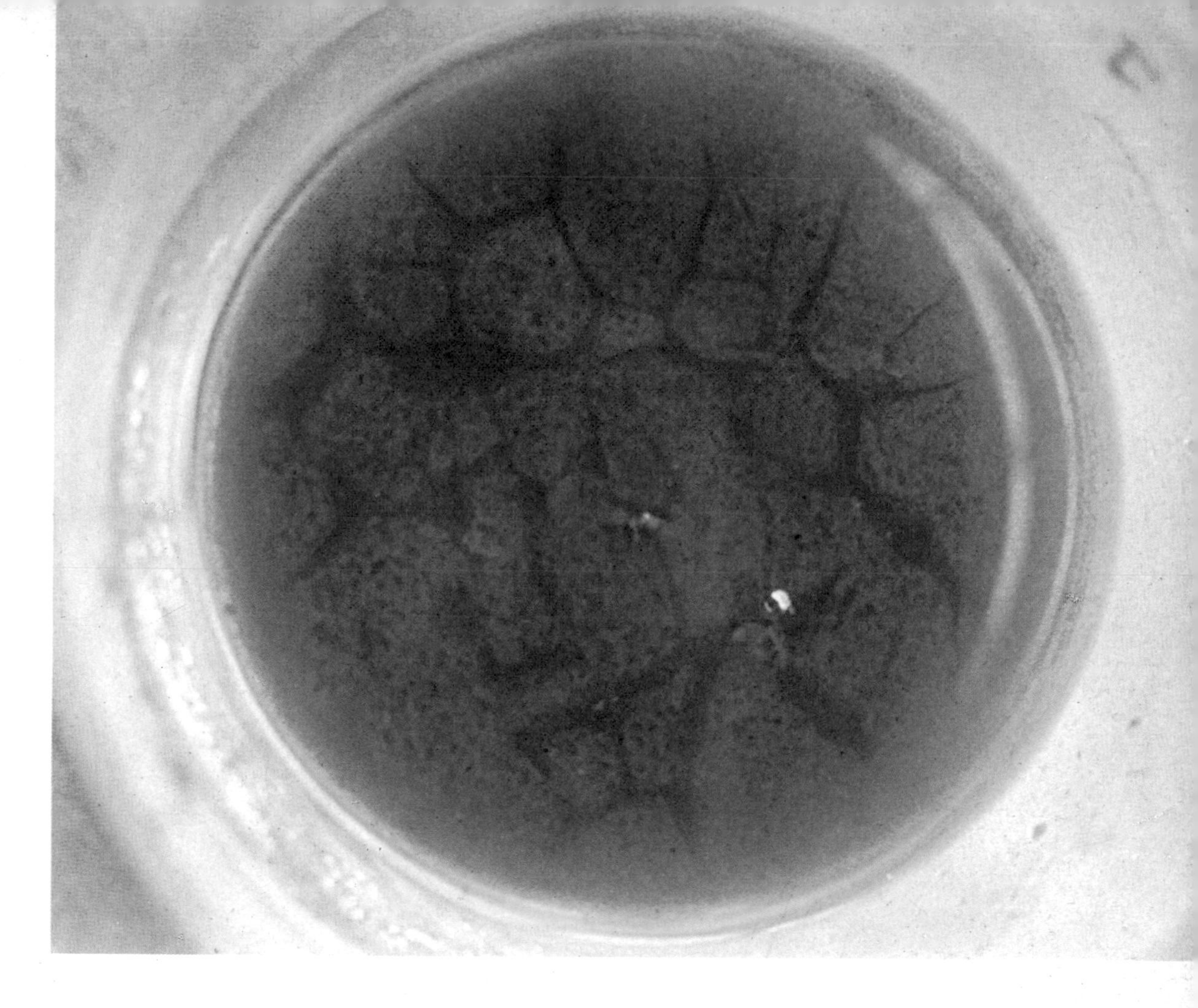

LEFT) Sir Macfarlane Burnet, virologist, immunologist and Nobel Prize winner.
RIGHT) Subterranean clover pasture research programme, Western Australian Department of Agriculture, Perth, Western Australia.

Australian scientists are exploring their many Antarcticas of human knowledge and understanding. Yet it is natural and proper that much of what we do concerns the husbandry of our own land, the practical usage rather than the abstract scholarship of science. This is both survival and responsibility. Study of disease in newborn lambs blazes a trail of discovery through nutrient-deficient soils to the famous "trace elements." Research in virology leads by way of myxomatosis to final triumph over a national pestilence.

I have looked and marvelled at electronically controlled synthetic night, falling over the massed green test-tube world of the Phytotron; and at a scientist "listening" to the

---

LEFT) Dr H. W. Bennetts, C.B.E., Western Australian pathologist whose research together with Dr E. J. Underwood, C.B.E., and the late H. R. Marston, pin-pointed the trace element deficiencies in Australian soils.
RIGHT, LEFT TO RIGHT) Francis Ratcliffe, O.B.E., CSIRO entomologist and Dr Frank Fenner, M.B.E., Professor of Microbiology, Australian National University, Canberra. Ratcliffe and Fenner introduced the myxomatosis virus to Australia's rabbit population.

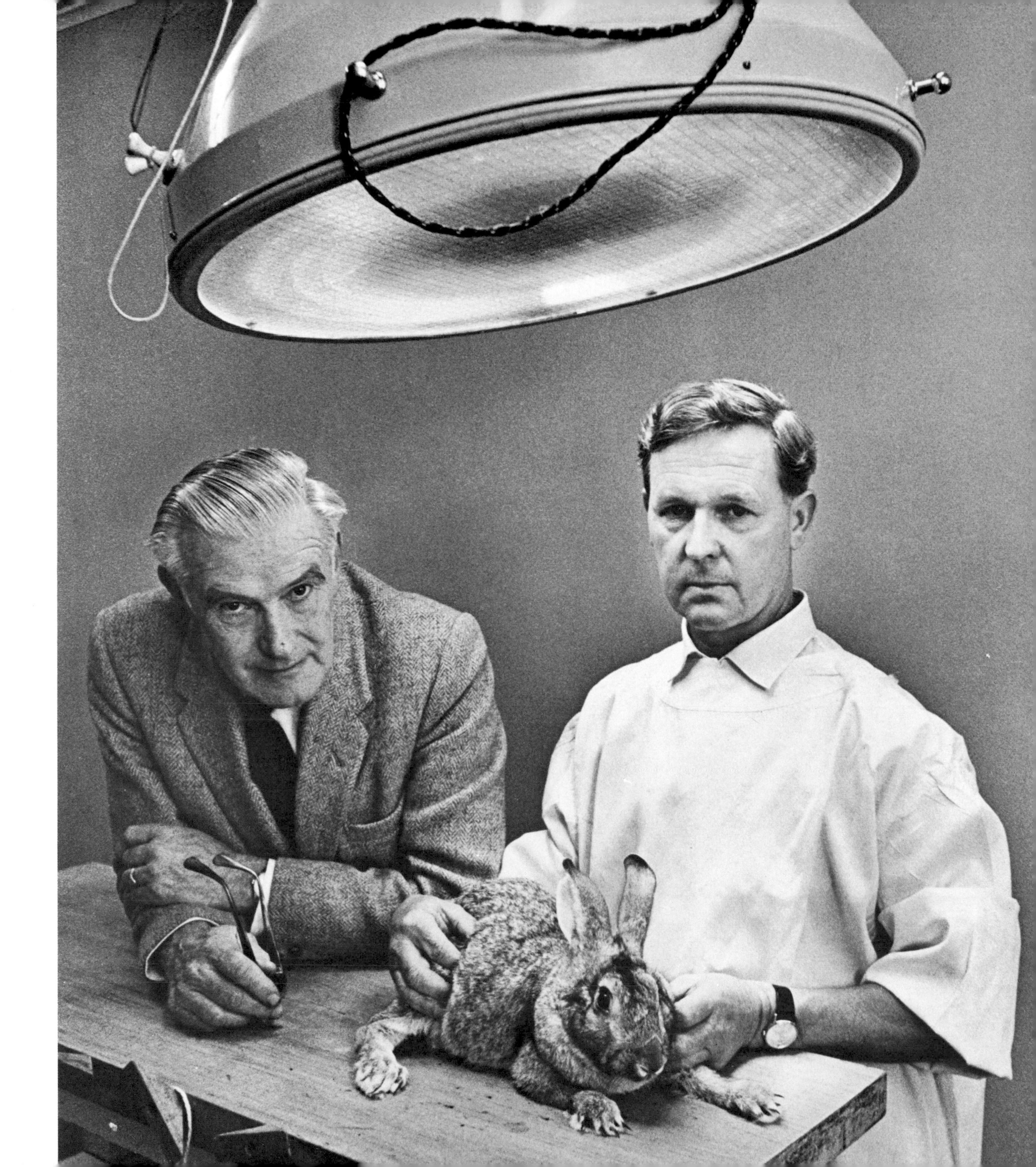

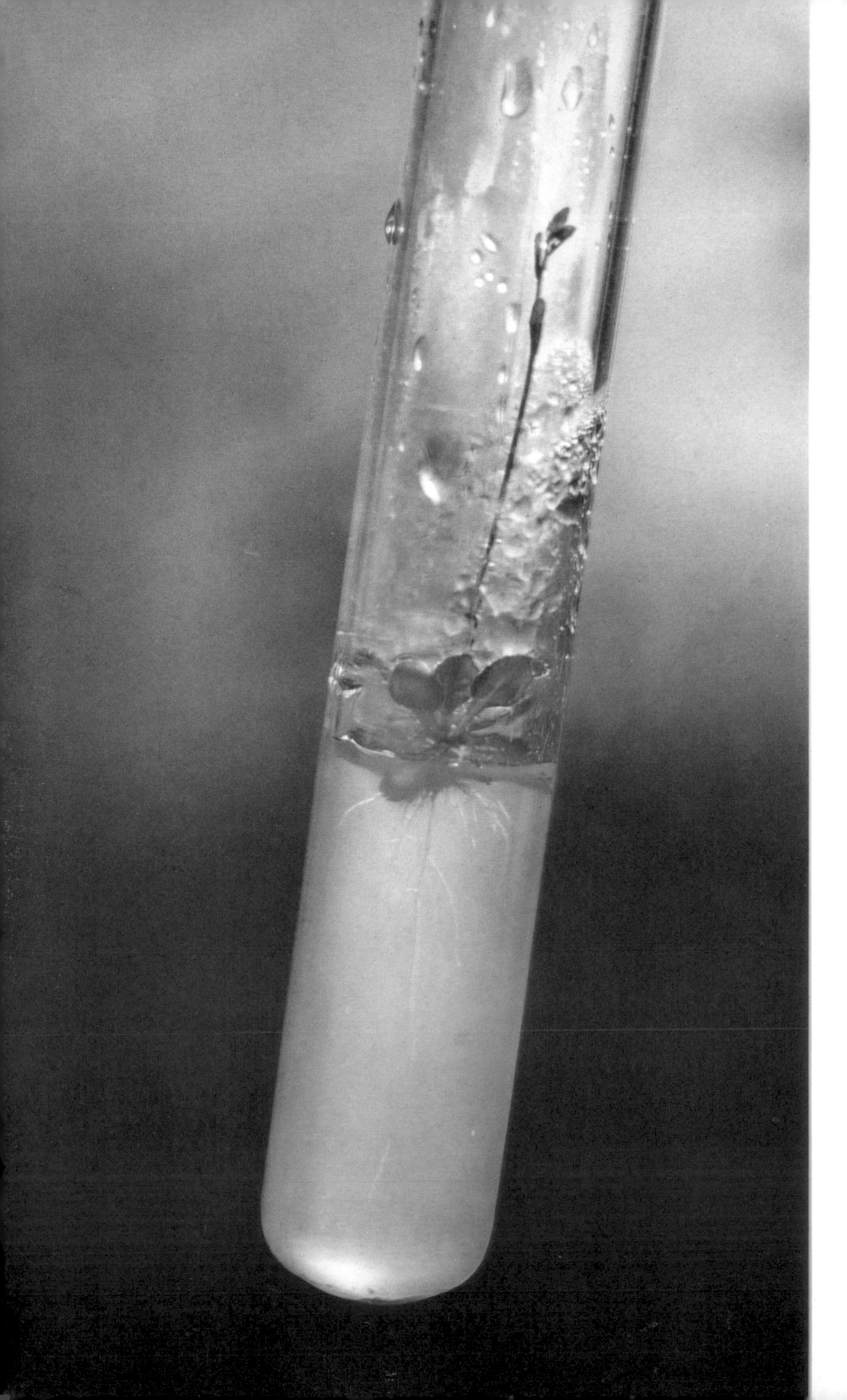

rhythmic respiration of a blade of grass. For we are concerned with the old mystique of earth-growth-season. And the Phytotron in Canberra – how does one describe it, as a superbly controlled gigantic, sterilised, electronic hothouse, or what? – is the laboratory where our scientists play briefly as respectful gods. One of them told me they call this titanic instrument Ceres, from the initials of its somewhat stuffy official designation: Controlled Environment RESearch.

LEFT) Plant genetics study, Phytotron, Canberra.
RIGHT) CSIRO scientist and wheat photosynthesis experiment, Phytotron, Canberra.

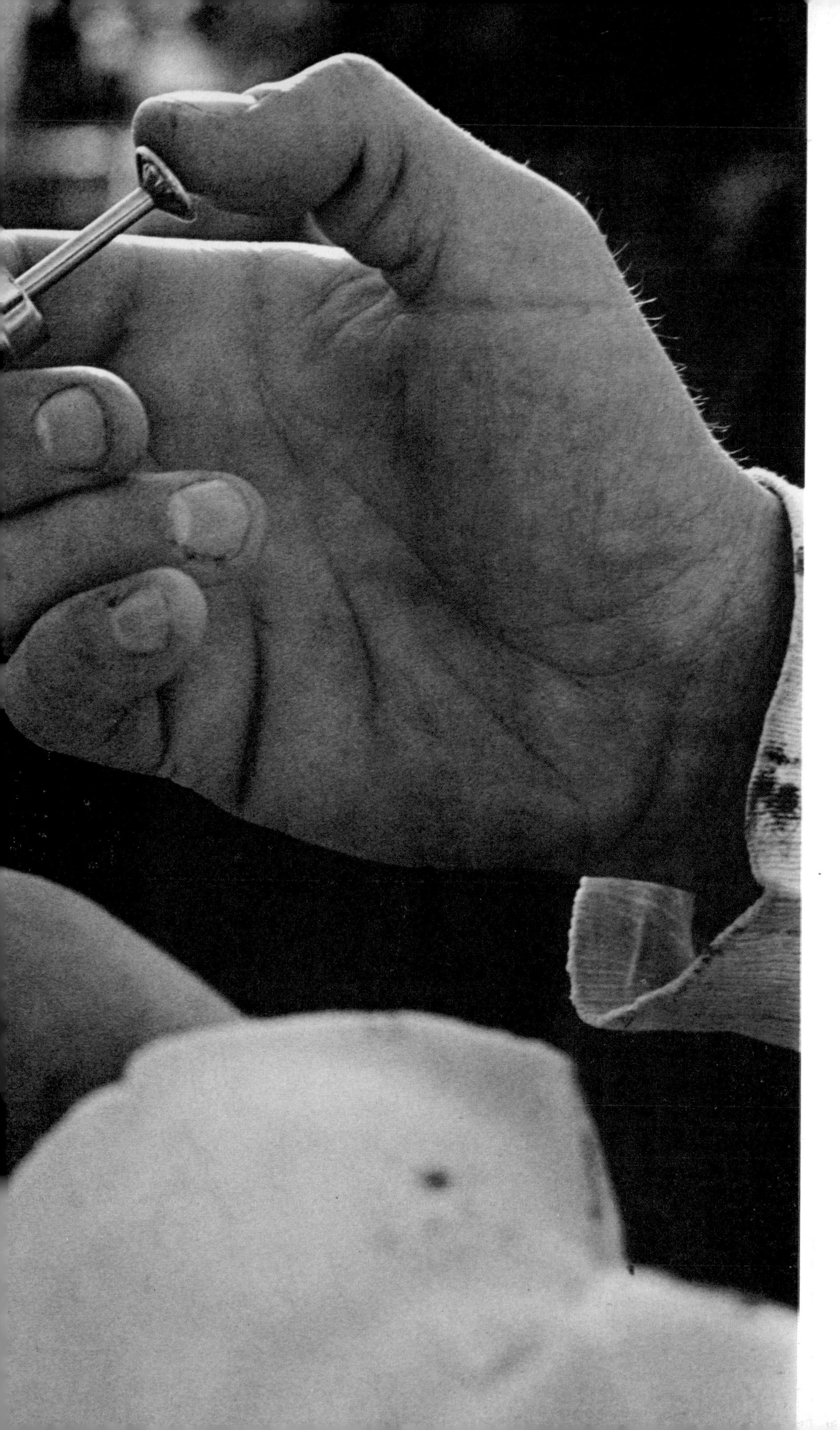

And all of a sudden there was that rich golden vein of poetry that is always beneath the rough skin of the land and behind our often unpoetic purposes. Ceres was the corn goddess, the fertility goddess of an ancient mythology. And I remembered one visit to Eleusis, not far out of Athens, where men performed for centuries Ceres' rites to the earth's fertility and the eternal cycle of life's regeneration. Yet this was Canberra, newest of our cities, and in a room of asepsis and fluorescence. In the foyer of that building there are words for us, appropriately cast in bronze: *Cherish the Earth for Man Will Live By it Forever . . . .*

There are two distinct Australias, an old and a new, and for the time being they are living side by side, sometimes uneasily. By my reckoning the new Australia is

LEFT) Phytotron research technician, anti-flowering experiment with antibiotics, Canberra.

exactly as old as the Atomic Age. We finally turned to face new directions in 1945, and since that was 21 years ago we and nuclear fission have come of age together . . . .

In 1945 I was with one of the first parties of Westerners to visit the ghastly fused horror of Hiroshima. That evening, beyond the grisly rim of holocaust, a Lutheran missionary who had lived there talked to me sombrely about mankind's "journey through tomorrow."

The other day in an outlying suburb of Sydney, Lucas Heights, I saw that we have already come a good distance on this journey. There, a hundred yards off the bitumen road beyond the scar tissue of development, rose the chaste, austere capped polygon of a structure that gleamed in the sun like some ancient classical temple or *tholos*. This was our HIFAR experimental atomic reactor, and near by the weird whirling universe of neutron irradiation bombarding beryllium oxide in another nuclear reaction. Here the scientists and

RIGHT) Computer and research technicians, Australian Atomic Energy Commission, Lucas Heights, near Sydney.
FAR RIGHT) Research equipment, beryllium oxide "Pebble Bed" nuclear reactor, Lucas Heights.

600 ml

students are pacing out the journey for the rest of us . . . .

We are still ruled to some degree by concepts which died beneath a mushroom cloud and by men never very interested in ideas, as such, and even a little suspicious of education and intelligence. There are signs of rush and stumble to make up for this, but still we suffer from under-financed and overcrowded universities, from shortages of good students as well as good teachers. Too often we grant only grudging support for scholars and scientists, who should not also have to be supplicants, and official policies of alms-giving are so parsimonious as to be startling in a land of so much promise.

Fortunately there are other Australian eyes which sweep wider

LEFT) Missile and satellite telemetry tracking antennae, Woomera, South Australia.
RIGHT) Technicians and "Long Tom" upper atmosphere research rocket, Weapons Research Establishment, Woomera.

horizons. They are looking into lonely or teeming places into worlds within worlds or beyond them – into the cryptic, crowded electron-microscope world of the virus, and the empty vastness between cosmic gas clouds beyond the vision of the mightiest optical telescopes, 10,000 million light years away.

We Australians have struck a bargain with these, our scientists. We have offered them our ample space for their telescopes, and even our vast barren interior as a playground for the lean metallic missiles that are the Damoclean swords of a nervous century.

But ours is a land which has a history of peace, underpopulated and, in the sense that much of it is untouched, underdeveloped. With what it would cost us to make a nuclear bomb we could feed an extra 80 million people. In return for the space and the challenge, we need our scientists' vision to show us entrance to and commerce with and a dignified equality in the late twentieth century world that we have so recently joined. For their arts can make the land for the first time our servant.

British Blue Streak rocket test-firing, Woomera.

The Arts

Among the ancient Chinese, esteem was based on an immutable scale that fixed all professions, crafts and callings in prescribed precedence. The poet and painter, the scholar and actor headed the list; the soldier was ignominiously at the bottom, only just superior to the public beggar. If a similar scale were devised for the Australians, it would be studded with paradox and surprises. True, the politician would occupy a very low rung indeed, with, say, the innkeeper, the government bureaucrat and the policeman. But the artist would be right at the top, challenging the supremacy of even the sportsman and the TV idol. This is the first paradox. Australians, who like to think of themselves as easy-going people, rough and ready, physical rather than cerebral, who are deeply suspicious of the longhair and the intellectual, also pay the greatest respect, homage and even, of late, cash to their artists.

There is no country in the world, not even in Scandinavia, where the easel painter of even reasonable competence can survive as comfortably as in Australia. Australians are great buyers of original art. Paintings are bought for various reasons, of course – out of genuine appreciation but also as status symbols and for investment. As a guide to investors, Sydney's leading financial newspaper has actually featured in tabulation a kind of artistic Dow-Jones Average of the country's painters and their current market appeal. But galleries and dealers enjoy lucrative rivalries, and top artists can have the incomes of successful businessmen.

Although bronzes are budding on the new buildings and there are stirrings of Medici-like patronage among the bankers and the burghers, sculptors are not yet quite so blessed as those pampered darlings of the Australian creative scene, the easel painters. And, although Australians are the world's greatest nation of book-buyers *per capita*, the lofty position on the totem pole of public estimation given writers does not often make their grip any the less precarious economically. Poets, like poets everywhere, enjoy esteem in circles where good poetry is esteemed and find it about as hard here as anywhere else to get their work published. Australia's first-rate composers share the poets' problem. There is said to be a desperate hunger for the great Australian playwright who will save Australian theatre, but there is no sign of this Messiah, and legitimate drama suffers.

Among the performing arts acting is, by and large, a depressed profession. But Australia's tradition of superb sopranos, from yesterday's magnificent Melba to today's *La Stupenda*, Joan Sutherland, waxes stronger than ever. The Australian public is unusually responsive to good music, and in consequence

Australia is favoured with some very good orchestras. One, the Sydney Symphony, is unquestionably of world standing. Public support is also strong for ballet, of which Australians seem by nature to be excellent exponents, and both ballet and grand opera are fairly comfortably, if surprisingly, subsidised. Going to opera, like attending art openings, is a social thing to do, particularly when the fare consists of such well-tested recipes as *Tosca* or *Rigoletto*.

All this adds up to infinitely more support for and appreciation of the arts than could have been dreamt of twenty years ago. And these two decades have borne striking new changes of form as well as popularity levels. Perhaps the epitome of these changes rises from a headland in Sydney Harbour, the site of the Sydney Opera House, called by the London *Observer* "the most important building in the world today." There are plans for an original all-Australian opera-ballet; the scenery by Sidney Nolan, music by Peter Sculthorpe, scenario by Alan Moorehead and Roger Covell, and choreography by Robert Helpmann. Signs are apparent of a powerful cultural renaissance in Australia.

Much of this has been forced by the sheer obstinacy of the creative workers themselves. There are people who have believed, and some who still believe, that the Muses never qualified for transportation to Australia, either free or bond. And until very recently, the arts in Australia have received only minimal patronage from government circles. This is perhaps understandable in a young and growing country whose politicians have enough to do without concerning themselves with the problems of the artist or the intellectual. Although probably apocryphal, there is the story of the local politician looking out at the end of a bush day with a grazier friend. "My word, that's a beautiful sunset," the grazier said. "Chop that sort of thinking!" admonished the politician. "That won't get you anywhere!" These are the attitudes against which the Australian creative artist has had to fight doughtily.

But the larger, more central and more worthy battle has been fought within the ranks and souls of Australia's artists themselves. For these Australians have had to grapple with the dilemma of a people desperately anxious to preserve and develop what is absolutely "Australian," yet equally anxious to be admired abroad and to compete on accepted international terms. Any country expresses itself in its arts primarily within its own horizons and for its own people. If it is lucky it throws up a giant or two who can be seen from afar. Independently, sometimes brilliantly, Australia has developed its own inimitable and highly interesting art forms; but there are a great number of creative Australians stubborn or valiant enough to want the best of both worlds.

In the interpretative or performing arts this is predictable enough. Dame Nellie Melba could not have been content with an ovation in the Monbulk Shire Hall; nor the Joan Hammonds and the Joan Sutherlands. Australian balletomanes in Melbourne and Sydney queue up to see Kathleen Gorham or Garth Welch dance, but what do the *aficionados* of Sadler's Wells have to say?

The same and other needs have also pulled Australia's creative artists overseas. And in effect it has been on expatriate battlefields that Australians have wrestled the devil for the possession of their own artistic souls. During the years creative Australians referred to as "the Frustrated Fifties," it was a common experience for "colonial" artists to go cap-in-hand among the European publishers and gallery directors and entrepreneurs. It was a common measure of their problem that in London Australians were recognised only as cricketers and in New York hardly at all. This has changed now, and publishers are rare who would close their doors to authors like Alan Moorehead, Patrick White, Morris West, Paul Brickhill and the late Chester Wilmot, authors whose books collectively have sold in the millions. Sidney Nolan, who once went for ten years without selling a single painting, has by now blazed a fresh, utterly Australian trail through the hostile ambuscades of international painting and won an immense new respect for the Australian creative image.

But these major Australians have confirmed and re-established an older pattern, rather than forged a new one. They have seemingly proved that some measure of detachment or removal from Australia, for a few years or for many, is organic to full Australian creative development. Only the poet, nourished by the resources of an inner privacy, can afford to be a stay-at-home, and the "travelling scholarship" has come to be the standard goal of any gifted young art student. Through the years this has been the artist's solution to his dilemma of Australianism and world recognition.

In the last century and for most of the first half of this century, the creative artist's first and often his only concern was to find adequate expression for an essential "Australianism." Through the early periods of settlement, style and approach in writing were merely extensions of English writing, with the novel addition of convicts describing experiences in savage settings. Theatre was an immensely distant branch office of Drury Lane. Artists in watercolours and oils dabbled away at landscapes, portraits and animal studies according to the European canon. Few were the men like John Lewin, who limned the strange difference of the Australian eucalypts, and like Conrad Martens, who fell captive to the effulgence of the Australian light.

The revolution came only after Australians took off and went overseas in the 1880s and returned with a whole new set of ideas. In 1889, the "Heidelberg School" – a yeasty, strong-flavoured group led by Tom Roberts, just back from studies in Europe and fevered by the new Impressionism – put on an exhibition in Melbourne of 233 Impressionist oil sketches all painted on the wooden lids of cigar boxes, every painting the same size, nine inches by five. The entire course of Australian painting was changed, for better or for worse, for the next two generations. These extraordinarily gifted young painters were a lusty, outdoor-living, emphatically masculine and very distinctly Australian bunch of people. They were the genre-painters of an unprecedented way of life, the meticulously accurate recorders of a new landscape.

With their contemporary writers, these passionate Australians defined and gave a soul to the Australian "bush" and the Australian image. They saw the light, the smoke haze, the dust, the gritty yellow roads, the hoof-pocked dams of clay and the untidy shagginess of the scrub, the heat-baked paddocks and the blue distances, the coarse-flannelled lives of squatters and selectioners and shearers and drovers and bushrangers and bullockies, the bushfires and the droughts and the clearing of the stumps and bracken in unkempt wildernesses. They saw it with all the love and dedication that Cézanne gave to Provence or Gauguin to Tahiti. They suffered at length from imitators and degraders, but they fixed a new and true and exciting Australian image that was to persist right through to the lordly white gums of Hans Heysen, Gruner's dew-pale mornings, the crystalline Centre of Namatjira, the aboriginal convert; even, in a sense, to the Nolans and the Drysdales of today.

In literature the goal, as purposefully pursued, had been the same – to give depth and definition to a new and different race of people living in a new and very different country. Like the painters, the writers were exuberant, masculine, openly chauvinistic, resentful of external intrusion, either by ideas or uninitiates. In the sombre, battling, sharing, poignantly human world of Henry Lawson's stories and poems, "mateship" and "having a go" became almost religious principles. The singing, surging balladry of the Banjo Patersons and Will Ogilvies, the wry but blatant xenophobia of Furphy's *Such is Life*, the simple, underrated rural comedies of Steele Rudd's Dad and Dave *On Our Selection* all contributed finally to the building of one great post-and-rail fence around the established Australian image. It was an almost entirely inland image, albeit one nurtured as fervently by the coastal dwellers.

Yet as time went on the Australians saw this as not enough. Their arts were hardly known outside the continent, and the continent was as far away as ever from the "real" world in which the mainstream of culture was presumed to flow. The Australians became conscious that they had, in a real sense, filed their own bill of divorcement. The acclaimed "Australian" works, the near-masterpieces and the big sellers, were being written by true expatriates – even by *non*-Australians. The writer closest to bringing off the anxiously sought Great Australian Novel was Henry Handel Richardson, with her fine trilogy *The Fortunes of Richard Mahony*. She was virtually a life-long expatriate. Katherine Susannah Pritchard's first recognised success came overseas. Christina Stead published nothing until leaving Australia, and lived abroad ever after. Miles Franklin spent the rich creative years of her life abroad. Here was another irony, another legend twisted on itself. The literary heroes of aggressively masculine Australia were almost all women.

Then, at the end of the 'thirties, a new wave of artists like Dobell and Drysdale came back from Europe with new ideas. In 1939 the Melbourne *Herald* sponsored a fine loan exhibition of contemporary European painting – and with one blow shattered Australia's creative isolationism. Here was an outside world of high creative art, upon which Australia had made hardly the faintest impression. From that moment began the movements which, at first gradually and then impetuously, were to alter – and are still altering – the patterns of art in Australia. That same vital year of 1939 saw Riabouchinska and Baronova and Toumanova and Lichine and Dolin dancing in Australia, with prodigious effect on the future of Australian ballet.

Thenceforth the leaders of Australian arts rejected blatantly exclusive Australianism. The old gods, though still worshipped in colour reproduction on innumerable suburban walls and calendars, gave way to Nolan's search for mythic figures in bizarre landscapes and Drysdale's moving poetry of brooding perspectives and lonely humans. Serious writers tried to shake free from bluegums-and-bowyangs in order to synthesise new originalities. In the rejection of the earlier and staled symbols – that gum-tree and sundowner image – there were violent if understandable swings to the pure uncomplications of the abstract, to Expressionism, to the passing fads of this Continental style and that North American way, to Pop Art and all the attendant hazards of succumbing to pitfalls of the derivative and imitative. But suddenly the smell of adventure was back in the air. Intellectuals were more militant than trade unionists, and there were more good painters in Australia than there were good jockeys.

Overseas, Australian art, no longer sealed within its insular amber, began competing and winning acclaim in the galleries of London and Paris and New York. An Australian orchestra was being applauded in London, and performing a composition by an Australian that was an homage to a Spanish poet. The Australian Ballet was on successful tour abroad, and one of the Australian-written ballads in its repertoire was a Japanese story. Joan Sutherland was back home singing. Adelaide's Bobby Helpmann, after 30 distinguished dancing and acting years overseas, was back with a deep new commitment to Australian ballet. All the talents and most of their visions were homing.

Everywhere within the arts the Australians are coming of age, no longer confined within their own horizons and encircling seas. They are still Australian, often distinctly so; but in a different, more honest and larger way.

But giants? Are there giants in the new landscape? On the difficult journey to nationhood Australia has surely advanced as far as America when *Moby Dick* was written; yet Australia still waits for its Melville – and its Hawthorne, its Thoreau, its Dreiser. There are some considerable writers and poets and at least one poet, Judith Wright, is very considerable indeed. There is a handful of talented and promising composers, two of whom, Peter Sculthorpe and Richard Meale, could be really important.

But giants? Certainly no unprejudiced judge of twentieth century painting would ever underrate the brilliance and stature of a painter like Russell Drysdale, the Walt Whitman in pigment of the great Australian loneliness; or of William Dobell, the sardonic classicist; or of Leonard French, of the enamelled jewel-like images; of strong-fisted Albert Tucker or Chagall-like Arthur Boyd; or of John Olsen of the *You Beaut Country* and the others. But giants?

If there are not yet giants visible – or if today's vision fails to see them – the Australians are at least now building a climate for giants.

IT HAS NOT BEEN an altogether easy country for the artist, whatever his field . . . .

When I was living on a small island in the Aegean Sea, Sidney Nolan the painter was also there, and within a comparatively short time so were his compatriot artists Cedric Flower and Carl Plate. Leonard French was painting on Samos, Alan Moorehead had been working on a book on Spetsae, Australia's best novelist, Patrick White, was living on Poros, sundry actors were passing through. There was a whole clutch of Australian painters and writers in Italy, a vigorous Australian colony centred around the Spanish Balearics, some painters doing well in Paris, and a whole regiment of artists and writers, actors and musicians, thriving or battling in London. When playwright-novelist Sumner Locke Elliott won the Miles Franklin Literary Award he was resident in New York . . . .

They had left Australia harried, and sometimes tormented by a drive to self-definition, or to know things older than the Nineteenth Century. There was an urge to measure against other pasts and presents and other people . . . .

There are many who still stay in the bigger and older centres of the arts, making their often considerable marks in programs and in the lights above the theatres, and in publishing lists and concert halls and galleries. Some find spiritual climates more benevolent than the dry winds and huge hot buffetings of their native land, and never come back. But most carry with them the live seed of their own country and people and poetry.

The stark bones and the blistered red skin of the Outback glare from the cool walls of the Tate Gallery, the weirdly-armoured Kelly emerges from the charred debris of Glenrowan on the walls of New York's Museum of Modern Art, the cadence of Australian music overlays the tide-lap of barges on the Thames's South Bank, the lyre-bird dances on the Côte d'Azur. But the ones who carry this powerful native seed do come back. More and more the cultured exiles,

RIGHT) National Gallery of South Australia, Adelaide.

the driven or self-elected expatriates, are returning to the creative challenge and ferment of their own country . . . .

A great flood of creative activity is building and spreading to all corners of our land. And it is in this fact that our true poetry lies. It swells past the hedges of suburbia, beyond assembly lines and the new blank verse of automation. Painters here are not only in the pads and flats and cottages of the cities, but scattered to the edge of the tropic canefields and the islands of the Reef, to the mountains and the old gold towns and cattle stations. The expression of what they are searching for lies on the canvas clean, bright, vibrant and brave.

A perceptive English writer has remarked on the exuberant vitality and young freshness of the colours.

RIGHT) Russell and Maisie Drysdale in his studio, Sydney, New South Wales.

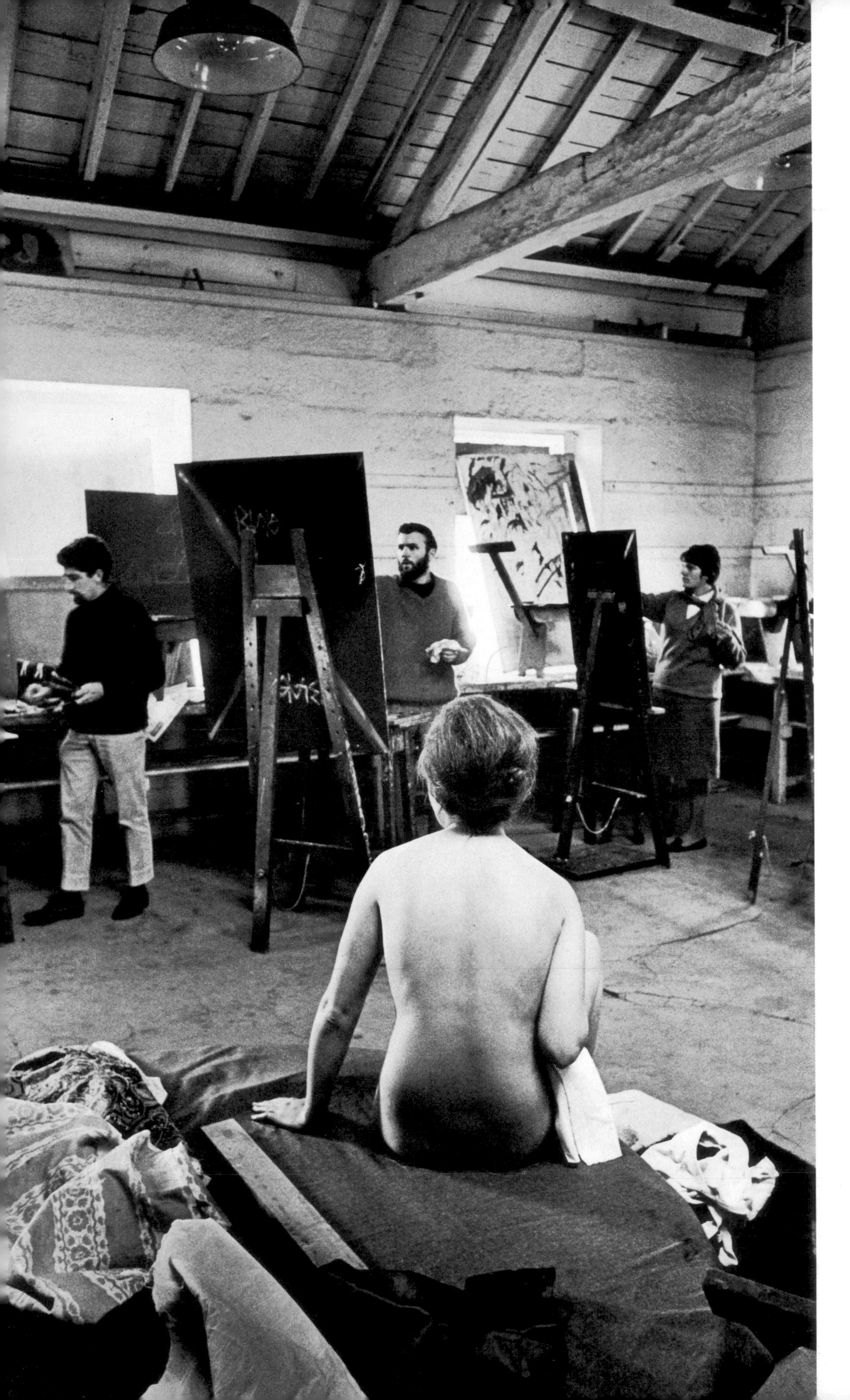

You hardly ever see an Australian canvas, he points out, that does not look as if the artist had at least *enjoyed* painting it. There is now a positive excitement in the whole field of the creative arts in Australia: it is young and living and energetic, in the act of growth.

The younger ones will still go away. It is part of the hunger and the need. They will come back in their turn, but sooner now . . . .

There are often discernible beginnings to things. The year I left school I had to stay home to mind my sister once while my

---

LEFT) Life class, East Sydney Technical College, Sydney.
RIGHT) Art student, East Sydney Technical College.

parents went off to see Pavlova dance. I did not realise then that this was the real beginning of ballet in Australia. Years later all the young reporters on the newspaper where I worked were attempting great leaps and *entrechats* and mooning over the then-visiting Riabouchinska.

I had almost a decade of art student life in Melbourne, and we lived in the constant swirl of tumultuous currents of ideas. We drew from the Venus de Milo or the Laocoön, argued about Norman Lindsay and the banning of books, ranted at the police seizure of prints of Modigliani's *Red Nude*, quarrelled over copies of *The Studio*. We clipped the coloured reproductions from the art pages of magazines, and wondered about Picasso. We were so terribly far away from where things were happening, in a tiny, frantic, intellectually isolated

LEFT) Aboriginal kite-hawk legend in Mime Class, Fort Street Girls' High School, Sydney.
RIGHT) Abstract painting in mime, Fort Street Girls' High School.

world, starving. Sidney Nolan had his first one-man show and a philistine flung a can of paint over his pictures. So, many of us left Australia to search elsewhere. Even Riabouchinska was not enough . . .

We are in a continual state of becoming. We are no longer a dependent continuity of the English arts, and we have outgrown our vaunted and aggressive insular nationalism. The real truth of that first visit by Pavlova lies in the achievement, 39 years later, of the

---

TOP LEFT) Dean Dixon, American resident conductor of the Sydney Symphony Orchestra.
BOTTOM LEFT) Peter Sculthorpe, composer.
RIGHT) Kathleen Gorham as Japanese moon goddess in Robert Helpmann's ballet, *Yugen*.

Australian ballet company performing Australian ballet at Covent Garden. It would be a bold prophet, therefore, who would try to predict the fruits, 39 years hence, of the cultural renaissance that sweeps Australia today . . . .

We are in a continual state of becoming. A jackaroo from the outback stations becomes an outstanding painter, a grazier outside Canberra and a diplomat in Moscow make their marks in poetry. A slaughterer in a Queensland abattoir shows his pictures in a Sydney gallery. So does a Broken Hill miner. A champion girl swimmer, practically born in the sea at Manly, gives exhibitions of the Australian crawl in Europe to earn money so she can study art, and comes back and

LEFT) Robert Helpmann, dancer, actor and choreographer.
RIGHT) The lyrebird scene from Helpmann's ballet, *The Display.*

founds a gallery, the so-nicely-named Hungry Horse, for the *avant-garde* of our abstract painters and sculptors. The son of a Melbourne tram driver, a fresh-faced pageboy in a pillbox hat who lives for week-end bicycle races, grows into the Sidney Nolan who paints the décor for Stravinsky at Covent Garden . . . .

All art begins with a blank page, a bare canvas, an empty stage, an unplayed chord, a block of crude stone. The sculptor, whether Donatello or Giacometti, thinks of a horse. Its existence is only in his creative imagination. All he has to do is cut away the stone until the horse is revealed. We are still cutting away at the blocks of stone, but the horse is there all right, snorting and prancing in our collective imagination, and one day

LEFT) Poet Judith Wright and husband, at home, Mount Tambourine, Queensland.
RIGHT) Mary Durack, author of *Kings in Grass Castles*.

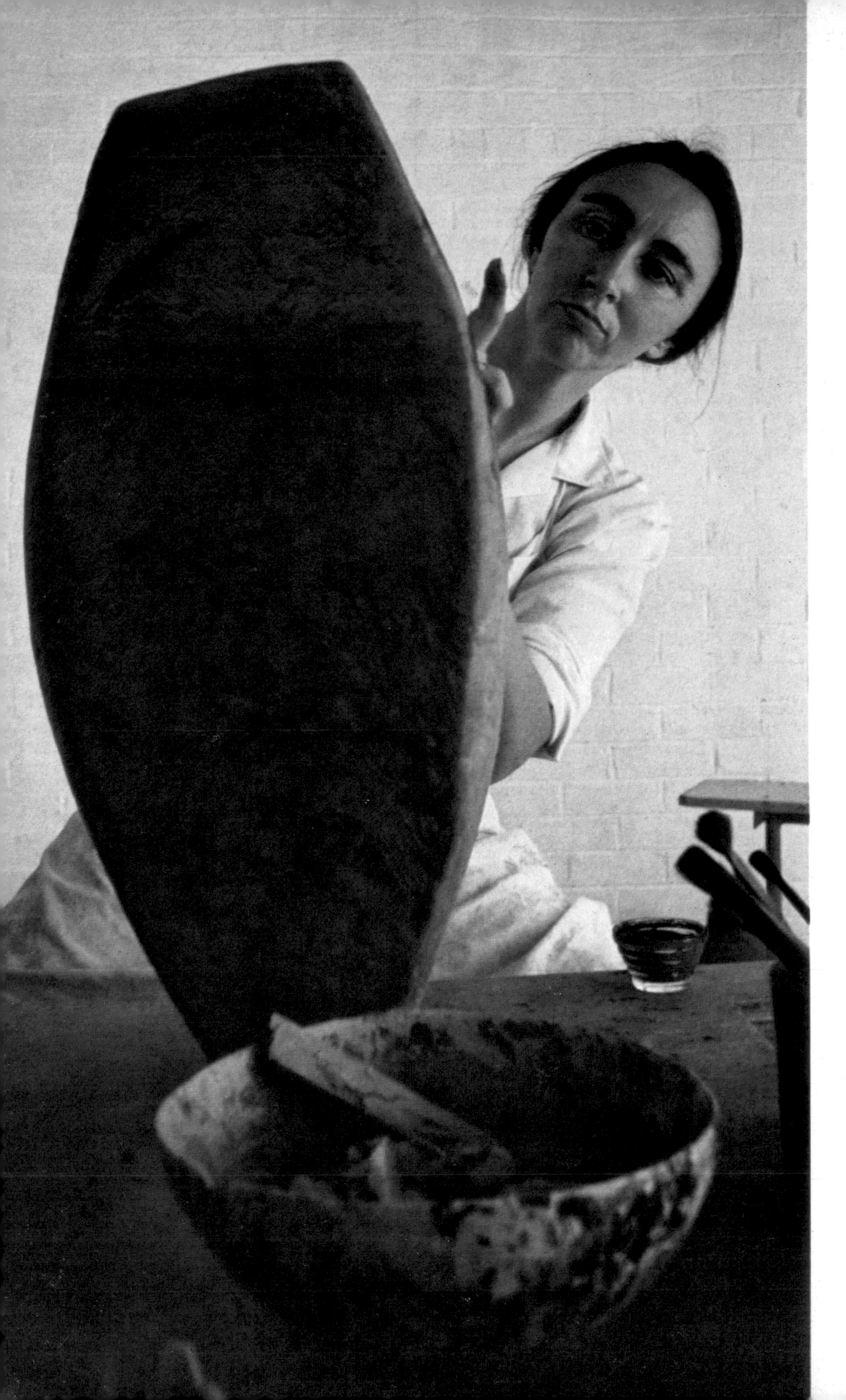

it will be there forever in the living stone. We just have to keep cutting away. Finding the shape. And this is the shape of music and pigment and choreography and bronze and the shape of ideas and images, the shape of ourselves and of our place in the universal pattern of things. This is why our arts are so important. They are all we have with which to define the shape. They are all we will ever have . . . .

Progress is an organic thing, not always planned or deliberate.

LEFT) Marea Gazzard, potter-sculptress in her studio, Sydney.
RIGHT) Soprano Joan Sutherland as Lucia in *Lucia di Lammermoor*, Her Majesty's Theatre, Melbourne, Victoria.

It is very possible that Australia, somewhat in spite of itself and to its own astonishment, is in the process of creating one of the great artistic wonders of the modern world. As the Sydney Opera House I think it is misnamed, but what does a name matter compared to the magnificent *fact* of its creation? It stands there on the headland off which Captain Phillip anchored the little *Sirius* when all this story was at its very beginning. It flings the great austere sweeps of its curves high and heedless above the petty acrimonies of the politicians, above dismay, scepticism, bewilderment and derision, almost free of all the old shackles. It is an accident occurring reluctantly, a kind of symbol. Yet if we achieve it, it will be the most sublime, daring, creative, and universally splendid thing we have ever done. It will long outlive all of us, and may even build us to posterity beyond our true present measure. A Danish imagination, and an Australian stubbornness to "give it a go anyway," built with the lottery money from a city's instinct to gamble, just there where Phillip came ashore and ran the flag up.

LEFT) The Sydney Opera House under construction on Bennelong Point, Sydney.

The Sporting Life

Cooktown, if you are going north up the settled eastern coast of Australia, is the last real town you will find. Deeply tropical, listlessly beautiful, it is a flavoursome place of easy camaraderie, some steadfast drinking, and strongly individual stamp. Most of Cooktown's characters are out of the novels of Conrad or Maugham, living in splendid rags on sunshine, pensions and the estuary fish in a kind of final abandonment to the Australian *dolce vita.* On Anzac Day, it is an admired German veteran of Rommel's *Afrika Korps* who stands among his erstwhile enemies and trumpets "The Last Post."

Among the landmarks of Cooktown is the famous Sovereign Hotel, half of which was once blown away in a hurricane, so that for many years, until procrastinated repairs were finally made, it was simply renamed the Half Sovereign. In this bar, when the stockmen are in town from stations 400 miles away and black "ringers" are in from the nearer cattle runs along with the men off the Reef fishing boats and the Cape York coasters, you can still see the Bull Fight Game.

In this exclusively masculine world the Bull Fight Game amounts simply to an individual pitting of man against man, not to display particular skills but only to prove masculine strength, toughness, courage or virility. The two contestants get down on all fours, and charge at each other head-first, butting skull to skull until one either concedes or is knocked senseless. Bets are laid on the outcome, of course, because of the Australian propensity to bet on anything; these cranial crashings are at least a change from gambling on far-away race meetings, the fall of coins, the run of cards in a pack, the passage of two bull ants across a log, or the colour of the barmaid's underwear.

Sport in Australia is seldom any longer reduced to the simplicities of the Bull Fight Game, of course; but these simple Cooktown recreational practices do embody much of the meaning behind the Australian's cult of sport and his rather extraordinary proficiency at it. A casual obsessiveness, if this is not a contradiction in terms, sums up the general attitude. In fact, the Australian's history and environment have put into his bloodstream a feeling for games and competitive sport which seems to be necessary to his fulfilment.

For Australians, sport is still predominantly a man's province, in spite of women's cricket teams, armies of suburban bowling matrons, and an apparently never-ending stream of "Golden Girls" of pool, track, and tennis court. When Australia was a masculine pioneering community, involved in conflict with a land and climate where victories were never certain and seldom easy, games or contests in which "a bloke had a chance to win" were agreeable if not imperative compensation for the dispiriting setbacks and failures. The acid pessimism in that phrase of very common Australian usage, "You can't win," with its despondent ring of futility, is still often applied to the land itself as comment on some disaster or catastrophe, to a sequence of ill-fortune, or to life in general. It is never used as comment on the outcome of a game or sporting event. Sport is the one place where you *can* win. In a masculine world, sport sits harmoniously with other activities of the all-male group – good-natured violence, mateship, the outdoor life, championship of the underdog.

In effect then, sport becomes an integral part of the Australian way of life. It has little to do with English beliefs that cold baths, rigorous games and the disciplines of teamwork are essential to the "making" of a man; the Australian view is that the country itself looks after such things. The more distinctive Australian attitude simply holds that a man should "be in it" with his mates and have a go at trying to win at least something – in a life miserly with laurels and offering no final or overall guarantees of success. Some of the results of this commitment to the Game are apparent.

Not long ago a leading American sporting writer said that Australia "is a land completely surrounded by water and inundated with athletes." He was moved to this glum comment by the tour of three Australian golfers (one of them a finalist in the gruelling U.S. Open) who had been cheerfully purse-picking the American professional tournaments that year to the tune of $150,000 or so. During the same week, however, there were any number of other events which might as readily have caught the writer's attention. In Europe an Australian long-distance runner named Ron Clarke was setting up 12 new world records out of 16 races; an Australian Rugby Union team was defeating South Africa's Springboks in Sydney while an Australian Rugby League team was defeating New Zealand in Auckland; at Wimbledon, in England, Australian tennis players were ruthlessly hacking their way to the women's singles title and to the seventh all-Australian Centre Court men's final in the past ten years. And another Australian golfer, Peter Thomson, was getting ready to win his fifth British Open and eighteenth national title.

In view of such performance, it is hardly surprising that in a number of foreign countries sport is considered the great, even perhaps the *only* Australian accomplishment. And indeed official statistics prove that in proportion to population Australia is well ahead of all other nations, including the U.S.A. and the U.S.S.R., in victories in international competitive sports. This has been going on for quite a long time. Australia has been winning international gold medals (over 50 of them to date) ever since the Olympic Games were revived at Athens in 1896, when Australian athletes from a land then holding fewer than four million people startled everybody by winning two of the track events.

The process began even earlier. Cricket had come to Australia in early colonial days with the English garrison. When the first visiting English cricket team came to Australia in 1861, Sydney went *en fête*, all business ceased for the day and Parliament was adjourned. A few years later the first Australian team visited England, an improbable team of full-blooded aborigines with names like Mosquito, Jim Crow, The Twopenny Tiger, King Cole, Sundown, Red Cap, The Bullocky, and Dick-a-Dick. The first white Australian team went to England in 1878. When England's great Dr W. G. Grace slammed the first ball for four, there was a roar of laughter at Lord's but Dr Grace was out next ball and in half an hour the whole English team was back in the pavilion. The match was a devastating victory for Australia and all England was stunned. Since then Australia has won 79 test matches to England's 65.

Tennis, like cricket, is an imported game. Australians have become world champions, and their record on Wimbledon's Centre Court has been staggering. They have won the Davis Cup more times than any other nation.

For no obvious reason, sculling is yet another field in which Australians have consistently achieved world dominance, both as amateurs and professionals. Since world professional sculling was introduced in 1896 the world champion has been an Australian more often than not, and the title at one time was held by Australians for well over 20 years at a stretch.

Add to these golf, swimming, motor racing, wood-chopping, dirt-track racing, cycling, almost the whole range of track-and-field athletics, polo, yachting, billiards, snooker and rugby football – in all of which Australia at one time or another, and sometimes frequently, has been the world's best – and the phenomenon has been established.

In search of his victories the Australian has plunged into the ragbag of other people's pursuits as if Pick the Game was a game itself; and he has scattered his continent with a welter of sports. Football is a case in point. Most European nations are content to play one kind of football. England, with 50 million people, plays three different kinds; the U.S.A., with 190 million people plays two. But Australia, with a mere eleven million people, has to be the only country in the world which fervently supports *four*, three of them imported and one indigenously invented. Almost every other game that was offered has been grabbed too, whether baseball or lacrosse from America, polo or hockey from India, cricket or tennis from England. The Australian has had to have a go at everything.

If facilities for competitive games were not there he has simply made them up for himself. The national game of "two-up" or "swy," needs only a reasonably flat bit of earth, a circle of male onlookers, the necessary contestants, some pennies to toss into the air, and a dedication to gambling and a lookout for the coppers. On the Gallipoli peninsula in 1915, when the Anzac legend was born, a vital element in the shaping of the legend was the passionate addiction of these young Australian soldiers to crude and improvised competitive games. In exuberant nakedness they romped and leaped and splashed and gambolled on a beach constantly under Turkish shellfire; the threat of death, normally present, merely imparted a thrilling extra quality to simple contests in cockfighting, saddle-me-nag, duck-diving, jumping, swimming, wrestling, running. In the same bloody and primitively heroic campaign, there were many occasions when a naked Australian in the forward trenches leaped impulsively from protected firestep to exposed parapet and shot it out in single combat with a Turk mounted on his own parapet, thirty feet away, until one or the other (and sometimes both) of the duellists was dead.

This goes to the root of the matter. The bush race meetings of today are the outcome of impulsive personal challenges between men of the Outback in the days of the horse. Even now in the Northern Territory a stockman will dismount and volunteer himself as unarmed matador in personal physical contest with a wild scrub bull. The need to *prove* is prevalent throughout the land – and although this need is often expressed before a critical and informed male audience, it is basically not an ostentation but a deeply personal acting out of the inner need to prove *to oneself.*

On the surface of it, sport grows more complex, more subject to faddish change and commercial exploitation. Bowling booms. Cricket, they say, is losing ground. Skiers flock in thousands to once-neglected alpine snow slopes. With the inpouring of Continental peoples, soccer expands to become a major national sport, adding explosive temperaments and uninhibited emotion to the arenas, and studding the results tables with the nostalgic team-names of far-away places; Polonia, Yugal, Budapest, Croatia, Triestina, Napoli, Wilhelmina, Juventus, Beograd, Panhellenis, Cracovia, Hellas, Kiev, Athena, Dalmatinacs, Malta. One day Australian soccer will surely avenge the ignominy of that record international thrashing, 17 – 0, at the hands of England in 1951. Australians grow bored by their own Wimbledon victories, but more than half a million play at night tennis or at week-ends just for the fun of it. And horse-racing is the biggest sporting industry in Australia. The turf programme uses around 14,000 racehorses and, nationwide, averages more than eight race meetings a day for every day of the year, a pretty deafening thunder of hooves by any standards.

Melbourne Cup, the two-mile race held annually on the first Tuesday in November, is such a national event that the whole continent comes to a halt and virtually every Australian has a bet down. But Australians don't need a Melbourne Cup to wager. Every year, according to the best estimates, they bet about $1,800 million, which is some 70 per cent of the total annual exports of the growing Australian economy. For Australians the Game and the Gamble are as difficult to separate from each other as they are from the national design for living. Even the Sydney Opera House, that transcendent symbol of a culturally maturing Australia, is being built with lottery profits – and probably never would have been built at all without them.

Some Australians have become touchy of late about the amount of national energy sport absorbs, and they like to point out that Australians in fact confine their sporting endeavours to week-ends and after work. The average Australian scoffs at any suggestion that he applies himself to sport with the dedication of, say, the German or the Russian. But to anyone who has seen the droves of tots being drilled on improving their backhands on suburban courts at week-ends, or schools of midgets churning the water under the watchful eye of a coach in a turtle-necked sweater and a necklace of stopwatches, the denial is not always convincing. Cynics are likely to point also to newspapers with their front pages splashed big with headlines about the marriage of a jockey or the transfer of a star goalie while news of lesser events like wars or U.N. crises is crimped to make space.

There are saving graces, of course, and these are as much a part of the Australian scene as the sight and sound of 100,000 screaming partisans at an Australian Rules Football Match in Melbourne. It is perfectly true that where the Spanish bullfight *aficionado* will throw his seat cushion when aroused, the Australian sporting onlooker, male or female, has been known to chuck a beer bottle. But no one who saw it could forget that when Jaroslav Drobny, that stateless man battling it out lonehanded in the curious cause of Egypt, played in the finals at Centre Court, Wimbledon, against an Australian, every Australian in the crowd was yelling his lungs out for "Old Drob." And the entire nation has rooted for an Italian or a Spanish team against its own countrymen in the Davis Cup, and for a team of coloured West Indians against its own cricketers.

Australia is the land of the anti-hero, the stronghold of the underdog. This, too, is an outgrowth of the Australian's history and environment. Because of the unique importance of sport in Australian life, the sportsman is sometimes among the very few privileged to enjoy temporary and qualified hero status, and sporting prowess is the *one* way in which even the female of the species can occasionally be elevated to masculine levels of approbation. Given time and after death, some sporting heroes might be admitted to a kind of shadowy statistical mythology, but none is allowed apotheosis in his own time. Suspicion falls, feet of clay are observed and the idol crashes. A champion footballer named Ron Barassi was once adored almost as a demigod in Melbourne, a veritable Hercules of the turfy oval. When, for pieces of silver, he left his own champion club of Melbourne and went as playing coach to the rival club of Carlton, the drama of "Barassi's Betrayal" threw a pall of doubt and misgiving over the great grey city's spires and towers, and rocked the very foundations of sporting beliefs and loyalties. Children threw away jerseys with Barassi's number on the back. Press coverage was enormous, of course. And the matter even commanded a good deal of space in one of the country's most important "little" intellectual weeklies. The incomparable cricketer Don Bradman received a knighthood a decade or two earlier, but never achieved divinity. Australia is a country without triumphal arches, with no Boadicea statue, no Washington Monument, or Lincoln Memorial; so the idea of a Bradman in bronze or an Emerson in marble would be laughable to the sports fan.

A horse is a different matter. Human fallibility is not an issue with a horse, it cannot understand partisanship, and would be oblivious to denigration. Moreover, Australians love horses. Thus, the most popular exhibit in Melbourne's National Museum, and a shrine for sporting pilgrims is the stuffed carcass of the immortal chestnut gelding Phar Lap, phenomenally fast in life, proud in purse-winnings, heroic in stature, and dramatic in death. (Did the Americans *really* poison him in California after he had won the Agua Caliente in Mexico in 1932?) Only he is justifiably preserved for the veneration of posterity, his great heart embalmed in the national capital of Canberra.

WE GREW UP WITH these things. They were always there, without being much thought about, and we just grew up with them – not sport so much, at first, as games. A wad of paper screwed up into a ball, a piece of beach driftwood fashioned into a bat. "French" cricket in the parks and tipcat in the back streets, and "ten and your taw" for cherrybobs and marbles and big-ring and toodalumbuks to teach us the excitements of gambling. Tiptoeing among the naked brown giants sprawled in the Men's Baths, and watching the 21-footers running with spinnakers from St Kilda across to Gellibrand, or the big A-class ketches reaching whitely down to Brighton.

Sport was something that was everywhere and natural, like summer days and seasons changing and Mother swimming the breaststroke at Point Ormond unperturbed by jellyfish, like dinking on bikes and going to school.

There never was any pressuring about it. We didn't even have a real sports master at our school. Old Kinross, the carpentry teacher, took charge of soccer because he came from Scotland; Crebbin, the irascible drawing master, had tennis and fancied himself in doubles with Perry from Science; and long skinny Jonesy, the maths master, used to lord it over everyone because he looked after cricket in the summer and "Aussie Rules" in the winter and yearlong had the biggest playing fields.

It would have been a very average growing up. One never thought anything particular about it. Because mine was in Melbourne there was Aussie Rules; in the bush there would have been games with horses, and up north the Bull Fight or woodchopping. Sport was the heady flavour of the world that surrounded us. We sat up at the radio half the night when the Australians were abroad at the Olympic Games or playing cricket against the Englishmen, especially if Bradman

RIGHT) Champion woodchopper Ken Jackson, Wamuran, Queensland.

was batting. On Saturday nights we rode the trams selling the pink issue of *The Sporting Globe*, with the last race results and the final scores . . . .

As boys, we went compulsorily to the sea baths to qualify for the Junior Swimming Certificate. We had to swim 50 yards and duck-dive for bricks, knowing that later, if we were good enough, we could try to win the Bronze Medallion.

We sailed little boats patched up with pitch and marline, made in back yards, most of them. Or we went into the three-mile Yarra swim, happy to come in 264th out of nearly 600 starters, finishing in darkness but with pride that one hadn't put a foot down once. We trained in the sea for the river swim, four laps back and forth over the three-quarters of a mile between Elwood diving board and the North Road pier, four laps even on the day Snowy Clarke, one of our mates at school, dived from Brighton Pier and was taken by a shark. They said that that never had happened before at Melbourne . . . .

When we got older we crewed in bigger yachts. We raced in one of the six-metres with a skipper who years later would contest an America's Cup, and there were others

FAR LEFT) Young sailing club member, Sydney.
CENTRE) Professional sailboat racer, 16 foot class, Middle Harbour, Sydney.
RIGHT) Olympic Backstroke Champion Peter Reynolds.

who had swum with us for the joy of the big Australian sea who turned out to be champions . . . .

In Cornwall, one years-later summer, at Sennen Cove just around the corner from Land's End, I came across a team of Sydney lifesavers demonstrating their rescue methods to an English group shivering in mackintoshes. It was rather like encountering a flock of emus on a grouse moor; nothing looked the same. It couldn't have been the same either to these big brown men who were circling the world to display their humanitarian craft.

For it takes Sydney's surf to give the real significance to these lifesaving teams and surfboat crews.

LEFT) Champion runner Ron Clarke on left, Olympic try-out, Sydney.
RIGHT) Junior league cricketer, Sydney.

Theirs are brave beaches, bold and brawny, with red cliffs and pale salmon sands and blue distances and storms assembling out across the Tasman, and the powerful beat and churn of that great surf, 50 miles of it around Sydney alone, always rolling in. This is a proper challenge for men who can row a boat 600 miles along a dangerous ocean coastline just to take part in a Queensland carnival, or freight the boat on a truck 2,000 miles across the dry desert to Perth . . . .

When I first saw the board-riders I had been away from Australia for nearly fifteen years, and this new sea thing that had developed among the young fascinated me. People were

LEFT) National Surfboat Championships, Collaroy Beach, New South Wales.
RIGHT) First-place team, National Surfboat Championships, Collaroy Beach.

talking of "the Surfies" and "the cult," of the stomping dances and curious rituals, and they talked with bewilderment, as if what was happening before them was out of their reach and beyond their understanding. I heard of Surfies with their lean hard bodies and bleached hair struggling by foot for days through the forests to the isolated and uninhabited beaches of south-western Tasmania, living on crayfish and river cod and rock oysters, carrying their boards on packhorses, just to find the perfect bay, the dream surf.

It seemed to me a paring down to a singular privacy of something that had always been with us, the same lure that led Eyre into the wilderness and drove Sturt to battle against the dancing mirages of the red Centre,

Surfboard rider, Avalon Beach, New South Wales.

old challenges in a new form, a re-shaping of continuities . . . .

Before the war we used to go to Buffalo and Bogong, Hotham and Feathertop, dreaming of Kosciusko one day, and these were lonely places of long runs and snow gums and here and there an isolated little cattleman's hut. But gradually the lithe brown men came out from the Vorarlberg and Switzerland, the Tyrol and Norway, and suddenly ski-ing in Australia had become *the* thing.

Once in Austria, when we were held up by deep drifts across the Arlberg Pass, we drank brandy in a roadside chalet with a ski guide and told him about Australia having winter snow fields bigger than Switzerland's and he smiled at this in courteous disbelief.
But five years later,

LEFT) Ski-lift, Perisher Valley, Snowy Mountains, New South Wales.
BELOW) Perisher Valley, Snowy Mountains.

10
ROBINS

he was out there as an instructor, and a few years afterwards he moved his family . . . .

When I was picked for a State schoolboys' football team we went across to Adelaide and stayed up all night in the train, sleeping in the luggage rack. It was my first time away from home; we were travelling into another state and we had blue jerseys with white Victorian V's on them and proper boots with studs and white laces. When the train finally got to Adelaide we lined up on the station platform for billets and a fine-looking lady with a veil on her hat looked at me and said to the team manager, "I'd like to have that dear little one there with the heliotrope scarf."

After that it was growing up, and club games, and liniment and rubbing-down tables and bruises and torn muscles and taking up tennis to play mixed doubles, and club smoke nights and socials and, just once, a vain shot at the Stawell gift . . . .

Much can be told about a nation from its institutions. Australia's two are Anzac Day and the Melbourne Cup. Most Australians don't know or care about the date or even the year of Federation, but they do know the date and year of Anzac. and *every* Australian knows what happens on the first Tuesday of every November, for this is the running of the Melbourne Cup.

LEFT AND BELOW) Participants and spectators, junior soccer team Gala Day, Manly-Warringah, New South Wales.

Special planes fly in from all over Australia, and milliners go mad. Almost everyone, including those few Australians who normally don't gamble, has "an interest." Anzac Day spreads its commemoration from before dawn throughout a whole day; the Melbourne Cup is the one happening of the year which for a given few minutes brings a whole continent to a standstill.

During the running of the last Cup I happened to be in the chamber of the largest bank in Sydney. Through its great marble halls a deadly hush had fallen, and everyone was clustered in tense groups around transistor radios. No sound came in from the streets; all traffic had stopped in Australia's largest city. There was nothing to be heard but the excited gabble of the racecourse commentator.

BELOW) Jockeys, Doomben Ten Thousand Race, Brisbane, Queensland.
RIGHT) Men's members enclosure, Melbourne Cup, Flemington Race Course, Melbourne, Victoria.

MEMBERS

And all over Australia it would have been the same, on Thursday Island and at the Half Sovereign in Cooktown, in the art galleries of Adelaide and the mines of Mount Isa, a whole people attentive at a tribal rite . . . .

In Australia, football is one of the things you have to take a firm line on. Rugby League. Rugby Union. Soccer. Australian Rules. There are no concessions. "The only game" to one man is "aerial ping-pong" to another. Nobody has yet worked out why Australia, where sameness in social attitudes is almost a national affliction, should be the only country in the world where four distinct and jealously upheld games of football have to be played.

The first code of football I played was soccer, but I had to give it up when I was about seventeen because my elder brother scornfully dismissed it as a "sissy game" and insisted I should be playing Australian Rules. We were living in Melbourne, the birthplace of "Aussie Rules," and besides it was tougher.

PAGES 256-257) Lady spectators, Melbourne Cup.
LEFT) Rugby scrum, Australia versus France, Sydney Cricket Ground.
RIGHT) Australian Rules football, Perth, Western Australia.

He made me throw away my shin-pads and for the next few years we played Rules together. My brother is now in his middle fifties and still limps slightly from old injuries . . . .

In Melbourne, football is a fever-disease like recurrent malaria, and evidently incurable. "Aussie Rules" in the austere southern capital probably has a bigger, and undeniably a more frenetic following than all the other codes in Australia put together. For six or seven months of the year a mad contagion runs through press, television, radio, and everyday life in a city of two million people. An acidulous Sydney man, himself a Rugby Union addict, put it to me that "Melbourne has no summer, only a period of hibernation between football seasons."

I had forgotten, until I went back to a Grand Final on the Melbourne Cricket Ground, what it was really like – that unbelievable roar of over 100,000 screaming zealots baying for blood and bruises, the toss and tumult of partisan colours, the streamers, the hats, the emblems, banners, frenzy, hysteria. No other sporting event in Australia draws a crowd as big or committed as this. Big, brawny and bruising, it is a game played on an immense elliptical field and even giants are sprinters.

LEFT AND RIGHT) Spectators, Australian Rules Football Final, Melbourne Cricket Ground, Melbourne, Victoria.

There are eighteen players on a side and the game is kept up, without time-outs, as long as humanly possible which amounts to four periods, each lasting 25 minutes. It is a cruelly hard game of physical impact, injuring constantly and killing occasionally, but it is considered effete to wear any form of body, head or face protection; most players disdain to wear even the sleeves of their jerseys . . . .

So, for a time, men become gods and heroes, my brother limps in his middle age, and I wonder how I ever came to give up soccer . . . .

Ron Barassi and team mates, Australian Rules Grand Final, Melbourne Cricket Ground.

Anzac

We have come to the end of the beginning. It has taken only 178 years – to breach an emptiness on the undercurve of the earth, to take a shadow and give it substance, to impart meaning to a whole continent, and to create a new people in the world. The time that began in chains and ignominy in an inhospitable wilderness has turned out to be better fortuned than the early auspices might have indicated. From a beachhead the Australians have battled to a point where they can begin to build.

The luck of Australia was its isolation. The distance away from powerful events proved an asset of incalculable value, for powerful events are generally powerfully disruptive and, for a fledgling nation, often better to be away from. Human record cannot submit a single other instance of a continent being free from war or bloody insurrection for such a span as 178 years; but Australia was left in peace to work out its own destiny, to build without particular impediment its suitable pattern of society, to create the laws and standards and the ways of its own free-chosen design for living, and, in peace, to concentrate on the task of the democratic betterment of an undivided people.

A handful of Australians, smelling the far adventure, have always volunteered for distant martial excursions, and marched to Kabul and Kandahar, and ridden to Khartoum and across the burning veldt, and in greater numbers climbed the fiery crags of Gallipoli. But these have been mercenaries of the human spirit; for the most part a world obsessed by bloodshed, insurrections, politics and greed for territories and markets left the Australians alone to look after their distant little affairs.

It was the bluff-bowed, frigate-built packet ships that brought to Australia, months after the events were over, the dispatches and broadsheets that told of bloody Napoleonic wars, of victories at Trafalgar and Waterloo. Clydeside and Liverpool clipper ships or square-rigged auxiliary steamers furnished belated reports on the Crimea and the American Civil War, or the Franco-Prussian War, or the great mutiny in India. The submarine cable and later the beam wireless told of Tsushima and Mafeking and human savageries that brutalised and bloodied every other continent on the face of the irrational earth. For these 178 years have been the most disastrous in destruction and loss of life in the whole long-suffering history of mankind.

Australia has been fortunate. The one war which did come close – World War II – came after the nation had matured enough to benefit from it rather than be shattered by it. The first continuous struggle to subdue the land lasted, in effect, from 1788 until the outbreak of that war in 1939. And then everything changed. Singapore fell to the Japanese in 1942, and with it the entire Australian Eighth Division and the shield of British power in the Far East. Short weeks before, Australian Prime Minister John Curtin had made an historic declaration that turned the eyes of his countrymen towards the United States, and established Australia as a Pacific nation and not an appendage to a distant homeland. It was the battle of the Coral Sea in May 1942, won by the American Navy, that turned the Japanese back from Port Moresby and Australia's vitals. Suddenly Australians became conscious that a sparsely peopled land would always be of interest to over-populated Asia. "Populate or Perish" became a dictum much quoted in newspapers and on the radio.

These events prove to have been the most important in Australian history since the coming of the First Fleet. Before them there was one sort of Australia. Afterwards there was another sort of Australia.

There were – and are – quite a few Australians who, content with all they had won, thought that the time of isolation could be resumed and enjoyed indefinitely, like some long, balmy, golden summer evening after a late afternoon shower. But the brief that was sound enough for the original penal colony – a place far enough away to be conveniently forgotten – was, and is, no longer valid. There is no distance left in all the world; even outer space shrinks with every hammering headline. With Russians and Americans wringing new science from the Antarctic and 2,000 million Afro-Asians finding new nationhoods, the far undercurve of the earth offers no more concealment. Isolation is gone, old shields have fallen, involvement instead of insularity has become critical to the Australian's very being, and change the rule of Australian life.

The most important and obvious change is in orientation. The stock is still predominantly British and Britons continue to be the biggest source of population increase, but the Australians are now a people grown out of their own peculiar environment. In this they have followed a classic historical pattern in racial development. The Australians are, in fact, one of history's great tribal movements in its vital secondary phase, a people broken away from the parent society that fathered the colonisation, changed according to the merits, exigencies and fortunes for good or ill presented by the new surroundings. Shaped by the ambitions of their place, they have undergone the mixings and assimilation of other peoples with the original parent stock.

Yet there are still Australians hardly aware that exile is permanent, that they have left home for good, that there is no going back to old days and old ways.

Although the world of Rudyard Kipling is in recessional as irrecoverably as the world of Julius Caesar, and from much of the world's map the pink places have vanished, they forget that dreadnoughts will never more patrol Imperial lifelines, and are unaware that Japan and not Britain is Australia's best customer. Although links with Crown, Flag and Queen grow tenuous, there are those Australians basking in the long summer afterglow who find such thoughts unpalatable. Others *would* find them so if they thought about them at all.

Yet these are the bald facts of the staging-post the Australians have reached on their journey. The Far East, the "gorgeous East" once held in fee, the East of the Raj and Durbars and the international concessions, of the Khyber's role against the "Russian Bear" and tea clippers at the Foochow anchorage, of the chunking paddles of the Irrawaddy flotilla and the white awnings shading the quarterdecks of gunboats, these have no reality now. For Australians it is not a Far East any longer, but a very Near North. The emblematic shape of the Australian continent sits rightly in its Pacific world – and there is such a spreading now of new links and involvements, and so many utterly new scenes unfolding, that it is almost as if primal Gondwanaland was, after all, only time's jigsaw puzzle, waiting to be placed together again.

At the end of their first 178 years the Australians have new and arresting responsibilities. Many of these have both a direct and a moral connection with Asia; few of them now have direct reference to any sort of control, even of a moral nature, from Britain. Even the Australian obeisance to intrinsically European patterns of culture – the "culture cringe" one writer has called it – is being shaken by native iconoclasms.

Australia is an autonomous nation, the only single nation to occupy an entire continent. In the islands it also has large and populous native possessions under its control and trusteeship, an area of 184,000 square miles with over two million coloured people. In the remote cold South it lays sovereign claim to territories hardly smaller than Australia itself, 2,472,000 square miles, almost half of all Antarctica, that polar continent that is the true and final *Terra Incognita.* With this vast range of present and future responsibility, Australia is still a land of few people. It is by its own decree a "white" nation. Yet Australians in the north of their country live only an hour or two from the outposts of Asia, and a farmer on the Ord River is closer to Saigon than he is to Canberra. Australia's economy is now vitally dependent upon Asian markets and would be plunged into deep confusion without them. The more the Australian continent is developed, the greater the need for Asian outlets for production, and the more pressing the need for people in the still-empty land.

This then is the general situation and dilemma in which the Australians find themselves as they move towards the end of their sixth generation. It is a time of great need for redefinition of what the Australian is, where he is going, and what he is doing about it. For there are hints of danger as well as reasons for self-congratualtion in the scene as it is now presented.

Australians are enjoying an unprecedented time of great general affluence and comfort. There is no real poverty; Australians have one of the six highest standards of living in the world. Perhaps as a consequence of this, the Australian in general is seemingly not as adventurous as he used to be, nor as individualistic. He lacks any particular direction, and finds it harder now to see where challenge lies. Blessed with most of the creature comforts that he needs for the good life, he more and more tends to settle for the easy existence, a remarkable development in a land that has never before made existence easy. His contentments spill over into complacency. He is quieter than he used to be, less aggressive, more conservative than radical, conventional in his habits, and unwelcoming of change if it is likely to disturb his hard-won *status quo*. There is a docility in the atmosphere never evident before. An extraordinarily large number of Australians are not entirely aware of the challenging excitements of the land they live in. Content with today, they are not conscious, or choose not to be conscious of the drastically different circumstances out of which other tomorrows must be fashioned.

Thus the new Australia of the post-war boom period has, paradoxically, superimposed several weighty new problems on those earlier problems that are still unresolved. The enduring problems are the aching dependence on climatic favour of a continent half of which has less than 20 inches of rain a year and one-third of which has less than ten inches, the massing of humanity in the few crowded coastal cities and the comparative failure of decentralisation, the critical significance of overseas markets to a buoyant national economy, and a population insufficient to handle the continental potential. In the past the Australian has always seemed to show up best in times of adversity; what is now to be seen is whether he can show at his best in times of affluence.

Elsewhere in the Western World this is also a time of increasing prosperity, even affluence; it is, therefore, no longer so easy to attract the migrants Australia needs for continued growth. Australia's birth rate as in other Western countries is gradually decreasing. Economists have suggested that the country can maintain its progress only by a regular intake of new settlers. They put the minimum need at 75,000 to 100,000 net immigrants a year and the maximum, to prevent disruption, at 150,000. Yet "booming" Western Australia, the State that seems most alluring to the foreign investor, still cannot get the population or the work force which it so desperately needs for its development. European companies have been obliged to bring in their own specialised workmen, some temporarily, some as settlers. Even Asian companies have brought in skilled workers from their own countries, and in certain conditions non-Europeans here on temporary permits can now apply for resident status and even citizenship after five years.

Both human and economic affairs have changed radically since the riotous days of the gold rushes and the Blackbirders engendered Australians' dread of "cheap foreign labour." Officially there has never been such a thing as a White Australia Policy, although Australia's immigration laws have operated to this effect. However, there are signs that changes are in the making. Many Australians look on their increasing involvement in Asia with mixed emotions. Japan is powerfully and prosperously industrialised, its cities and its urban way of life at least as sophisticated as Australia's. As likely as not the music floating peacefully over the sybaritic pleasures of a sundrenched Australian beach comes from a Japanese-made transistor, and the young man's surfboard may well have been carried there on the roof of a Japanese car. Japanese ships carry away Australian wool, iron ore, bauxite, and coal, much of it won from investment by Japanese industrialists; bulk carriers load more Australian wheat for a Chinese Republic (which it does not recognise diplomatically) than for any other export market. Australian commitments to SEATO and the ANZUS pact are underscored by the fact of Australian troops fighting alongside Americans in South Vietnam and alongside Commonwealth forces in Malaysia. The frontiers of Australia's entrusted New Guinea territories are also the frontier of Indonesia's West Irian. For the QANTAS jet airliners flying out of Sydney the cities of Asia, only a few hours away, are the first stopping places on Australia's world air routes. Under the Colombo Plan and other schemes, there are more than 12,000 Asians, mostly students, temporarily living in Australia to learn from Australians about many things that Australia can teach them. There are *not* 12,000 Australian students living in Asia to learn many things that Asia could teach them.

The presence of the Asian students and the eager, ready acceptance of them by Australian students (the one numerically strong body best oriented to new directions) are, none the less, harbingers of change. Australian artists and intellectuals, too, are increasingly interesting themselves in Asian themes and tableaux and are progressively more impatient with old shibboleths.

Officially there is yet no clear-sighted declaration that the Australians must find some way of living with the Asians; nor, indeed, even a pretence of submitting any possible alternative. Intelligent public opinion – and there are a great many intelligent, tolerant, humane, and forward-looking, if, alas, rather inarticulate Australians – tends to think in advance of the politicians. If the public opinion polls are not to be discounted, there already exists a firm majority of Australians who are hopeful for new, deeper relationships with an emergent Asia already suggested by recent modifications of Australia's immigration policies. And these continuing attitudes are essential preconditions for an Australian future of true wealth, variety and realism.

In the forming of new attitudes, the national dichotomy goes deep. There is that prevalent type of Australian, usually but not necessarily of an older generation, who is inseparably bound to the conditioned attitudes and *mores* of a vanished time. No other people in the world, for example, can match the Australians' propensity for wearing badges which signify, among other things, participation in wars that ended 20 years and even 46 years ago. The curious paradox is that the badge-wearer would be the last, for fear of being thought a "skite" or "bull artist," to boast of imaginary, or even real, exploits in those wars. It is this Australian, loyal to the cliché in everyday conversation, who is most inclined to cling, as for self-preservation, to clichés of conduct and attitude.

The crisis of this contemporary Australian is that he may be unwittingly the slave to an obsolete image. He can be a timid fellow and see himself a swashbuckler; the taciturnity of the old bushman he converts into a studied inarticulateness; long-ago heroisms provide him with a continuing spiritual comfort in the conviction of his own heroic qualities if put to the test; carried to the extreme of image-assertiveness he can be a city man born and bred who will travel to Europe wearing a "Digger" slouch hat turned up at the brim and with a kangaroo and the Southern Cross boldly painted on his baggage. The saddest thing about him is his inability to see that he does not have to flaunt or prove his unmistakable Aussie-ness, that the record of his people no longer calls for self-advertisement. He is big enough now to be taken on his merits.

Yet his is the type that strengthens the forces of reaction in a time of enormous and critical change. Unconsciously he epitomises all the Australias that have formed him: he stands, a firm and strong man, with one foot in a hard past and the other in a comfortable but baffling present. Trade unionists, who fought so valiantly for an eight-hour working day and eventually got it, march now, beneath brave banners but not very truculently, for a six-hour working day which automation is bound to give them anyway. In a land which paradoxically has both a rich abundance of leisure and a dearth of labour for the work that must be done, the dictation of an early masculine society continues to impose both social and economic inequalities on women. Although the economy needs all the brains and ability and working energy it can get, there are still quarters where married women going out to work elicit disapproval, and when she does work, even in the same job as a man, the woman is frequently paid less. Little acknowledgement is made of the evident fact that many women in their chosen fields are at least as capable, efficient and industrious as the man, and on the whole are better read, have a wider tolerance and a more instinctive awareness. The Australian wife is probably more "spoilt" by her man and domestically more comfortable than wives elsewhere, but she has paid for these indulgences by some loss of spiritual independence, many weaknesses in her emancipation and a comparative lack of worldly sophistication. This is a pity, for the Australian woman has a wonderful vitality and an exuberant animality and quick intelligence that should not be confined by suburban hedges. One of the predictable changes in Australian life must be the wider sharing of social and public life between men and women, and the erosion of the comforting but limiting thought that a jug or two of cold beer with the boys and the kids healthy and properly looked after are about as much as a man has a right to expect out of life.

A comparison might be made with the pagan society of classical Greece which was also a predominantly masculine society where women were restricted to domestic affairs, where there was great devotion to outdoor living, obsession with games and sports, a love of gambling, and a great emphasis on physical and martial prowess. But there the similarity ends.

But to judge Australians by this group alone would be rather like judging the British by only a cursory examination of "The Establishment." It does not, for one thing, take into account the great gap that now divides the generations. Australia is a very young country in more ways than the one customarily used to excuse shortcomings: five and a half million Australians, roughly half of Australia's people, are not yet 30 years old. The Australia they have grown up in is altogether different from the Australia of before the war. They live in a prosperous time, and are on the whole both better educated and more intelligent than any previous generation of Australians. But they are inclined to rattle round loosely in the great space, some of them unhappy without quite knowing why, others anxious for redefinition or some definite new goal to aim at or image to cling to.

There is also now a very considerable body of migrant people, some two million of them, who, nurtured in other civilisations and other societies, can hardly be expected to understand the strange and exotic rites, shibboleths and sacred cows of their adopted land. Some of their cosmopolitanism has rubbed off on native-born Australians – and rubbed away some of the old prejudices.

There is a third group which, although it does belong to the older generation of Australians and understands and respects the images upon which it was fostered, is also conscious of the climate of sharp change and the urgent need for national reassessments. Their numbers are uncertain, but they include a fair proportion of the intellectuals and creative people, returned expatriates, quite a number of the more enlightened and adventurous businessmen and industrialists, a large number of scientists (many of whom are of foreign stock anyway), a sprinkling of academics, as well as some quite ordinary citizens. This group includes the most vocal and questioning people in the land.

Together these three groups outnumber the reactionary and conservative element. If they are not yet united in any clear vision – either of opposition or of advocacy – they do share an iconoclasm which must precede further great change in the Australian landscape, internally as well as externally. These groups – and the rampant technologies of our time – have already compelled many changes, of course. In many respects the Australians have changed more in the last ten years than in the previous 50 years, that period in which the significant "Anzac Legend" had its birth, the bushranger Ned Kelly achieved apotheosis as a demigod, and "the bush" was taken to the city's heart. They will change far more in the next ten.

Two of the more pronounced phenomena of recent years ensure this progress: one is the rise of the young man in positions of authority or executive responsibilities and the other is the almost fanatical new obsession with higher and broader standards of education. Australia still lags well behind such leaders as Japan, the U.S.A. and Britain in the provision of university facilities and in the number of first year students. The 21,528 new students in all Australian universities in 1964, although not even double the number of Asian students present in the country at the same time, nevertheless will have more than doubled within the next ten years. Everywhere there is a frantic building of new universities and of extensions to old ones. To see today the packed lecture halls in the Australian universities, the students swarming in the high schools, the young executives and young scientists and young leaders in public life, is to realise that the future of the country is already passing into different hands.

There is not only a greater political and economic orientation towards the United States, but many of the common patterns of living are being drawn directly or adapted from American patterns. New concepts in business methods and management, in advertising, in public entertainment and recreation, for all the "Australianism" underneath, would strike a more responsive chord with the American visitor than with the English. It is another of the Australian paradoxes that a people so reluctant to accept change in many of its social and moral attitudes accepts technological change so readily, eagerly, and so efficiently. Book censorship continues and it has taken until recent times for Australia to amend its old-fashioned liquor laws and social drinking patterns. These patterns, with the men and women still largely separated, invariably raise the eyebrows of overseas visitors. But these same old-fashioned folk support many more television networks with their eleven million people than Britain does with 50 million; they run more motor-cars, use airplanes more frequently, have altogether higher standards of domestic comfort and more of the mechanical aids to "modernisation" in their daily lives than any people except the Americans.

All these are aspects of the present pattern of rapid change, in which the young generation of Australians will play an ever more important role. For all the impact of technology, this is the quintessence of Australia's inner struggle today – a tension between generations.

In the post-war years one of the most significant moral conflicts between the old and the new generations has pivoted around the Anzac or "Digger" legend, which commemorates the Gallipoli invasion in 1915. To the older generation Anzac is the fitting and sacred symbol of the heritage of nationhood. Many of the younger generation argue that the Anzac story has been both romanticised and despoiled, that it concerns events too far back in time and too far away in distance to worry about. To them Anzac has little application in an age when overseas combatants are no longer necessarily volunteers and in which, for the first time in its history, Australia has "a neighbour problem."

As always there is something to be said for both sides. Anzac Day is the one day of the year commemorated the length and breadth of the land, the truest national day of Australia, a land which more than ever needs its sense of nationhood. Anzac is the one celebration which has a core of deep and genuine spiritual feeling. Over and above all it exalts courage, the same sort of courage that won the land from the dry red fastnesses in the first place, that triumphed over adversities, that built a proud nation out of impossible beginnings; the sort of noble human courage that has always been useful and admirable, and will be useful and admirable again.

By a series of accidents, chances and causes now no longer important, thousands of young Australians and New Zealanders, virgins in battle from distant lands which had never known war, were flung against the forbidding beaches and cliffs of the Gallipoli peninsula on 25 April 1915. With splendid audacity they scaled supposedly impossible crags, dug themselves in on the fire-swept heights, and stayed there on the ravaged Anzac beachhead for over eight months under almost constant bombardment from the Turks and appalling conditions and privations. Despite ghastly casualties they were never dislodged.

Here we have, simply, a military exploit – one on the grand scale, admittedly, and classic in terms of human courage and endurance – but this is not the Anzac legend in its true essence. What became legendary, what startled, without exception, every foreign observer who visited the Anzac beachhead between April and December of 1915 was the extraordinary demeanour and unique spirit of these callous, cynical, carefree young soldiers from half a world away. They seemed to belong, not to the standard conceptions of military prowess and disciplines, but to some other, younger, more exuberant world of the spirit. Physical, masculine, their big sunburnt bodies remarkable to an older world, they romped naked under shellfire on the beaches and even fought naked in their clifftop trenches. Activated by simple codes of loyalty, adventure, and comradeship, they seemed unmoved by, even sceptical of any thoughts of jingoism or patriotism; they admired and respected "Johnny Turk," the enemy, far more than they ever admired or respected their own leaders. The Anzacs were to all outside observers a remarkable new breed of men. Poetic observers such as John Masefield, Compton Mackenzie and Sir Ian Hamilton even saw them as the reincarnation of the ancient Trojan heroes.

As the campaign went on with its wild and senseless carnage, involving a million men of whom more than half, more or less equally divided on either side, were to become casualties, the legendary status of the Anzac grew. As the stench of an almost unbearable summer passed into the bitter cold and the stark realisations of winter, and as the disheartening awareness of the grim and ghastly nature of the Gallipoli bungle spread, only the spirit of the Anzacs appears to have survived unimpaired. Over and above the total grimness of war, and overriding both heroics and histrionics, was a very peculiar sense of humour which only the Australians seemed to possess. Sardonic, self-denigrating, often macabre, it placed war, and all the horrors and perils that go with war, on a plane *below* human reaction to it. By a curious self-mocking emphasis on the human predicament, it managed to sublimate the predicament in man's spirits.

This was the very essence of the spirit of these young men and of the far-away land that had shaped them in its mould, and this became the stuff of legend. Perhaps Australia erred in trying to take the fine and delicate thread of this story and weave it into the tough rope of purely national heritage or tradition. What was clear half a century ago is not seen at all clearly now – that a true legend simply *is*. It belongs outside, and transcends historic sequence or even significance. It exists in its own time, lit by its own inner radiance and standing not for mere nationalism but for the universality of the human spirit.

The event of Anzac ended strictly with the evacuation of Gallipoli, just as the event of Hector and Achilles ended with their own deaths and the sack of Troy. A legend is complete with its own completion. Strings cannot be attached to drag it along through historic continuities, as a hanging line for messages and moralities and homilies. The military exploit can be commemorated nationalistically – that heroic storming of foreign cliffs that fused a people into a nation in a furnace of fire and sacrifice. But the legend that transcends the exploit is not for a nation to commemorate; since it is of the human spirit it belongs to all mankind.

The Anzac legend, however, derives from something nearly unique in Australian character and instinctively seems to transmit itself to Australian character. The Australian writer Ken Inglis has said that in the commemoration of the dead in the Anzac monuments, the appeals are not to Christianity but to the stoic view of life as an heroic ordeal. In drawing on this observation Donald Horne, another Australian writer, has touched truth when he says, "Australians have long both understood the inadequacies of action and at the same time enjoyed action. They know how to be heroes without a cause, to suffer ordeal sardonically, to accept rules in which they do not finally believe. The Australian is both sardonic observer and cheerful participant."

Perhaps, after all, there is less reason for incompatibility between the generations than is generally admitted. The same wry, self-mocking humour of the Australian soldier in the Second World War, and with it his acceptance of the "heroic ordeal," was very evident in the Western Desert and New Guinea. It was never any platitudinous "inheritance of the Anzac spirit" – as if the legend was something to be handed on like a used coat or a family heirloom – but simply part of that same inherent quality in the man that was displayed for the first time and under such fantastic conditions on the cliffs of Gallipoli. Here was the stoic and almost pagan attitude of acceptance of the ordeal as a test of fibre and, above all of man's ability to laugh at the absurdity of a situation he found himself in – even when the absurdity had the stench of death about it.

It is to be hoped that in a new time and in the face of a new challenge the Australian will not lose, or himself trade in for transient comforts and consolations, these rare and important qualities. If the legend of Anzac is seen for what it *is* and not just what it is *supposed* to represent, it can unite all today's Australians and furnish a lasting beacon in the most exciting and challenging time the Australian people have yet known.

APRIL IS AUTUMN IN AUSTRALIA. The air is cool, even in the wet latitudes of the Queensland coast where the Great Barrier Reef threads a sea afloat with islands called Daydream and Happy Bay. To the north-west, towards the channel country and the huge empty Northern Territory, the hammer heat of summer is gone. South towards the lower end of the continental island the air is sharply colder, and dawn risers, thin-blooded from summer on beach or inland plain, will shiver as they dress in dark suits or quiet frocks and sometimes ageing uniforms.

Anzac Day begins before dawn. In the cities, shapes begin building in the dark hours soon after midnight. Men and women, mostly elderly, come singly or in couples until they are a crowd and then a congregation waiting for the dawn. There is little talk. Sometimes the breathing silence is shivered slightly by the hiss of a match as an old soldier surrenders to his tobacco yearnings, or a shoe scrapes to ease a creaking joint. Here and there a shadowy figure walks tentatively along the edges of a group in search of an old wartime mate, a sister who did not marry.

Outside the cities the darkness is thicker. The bush – vast, brooding, barely peopled – lacks the glow that warms the edge of a city no matter how deeply it sleeps. Here in the country towns Anzac Day begins with a small quiet assembly, a lonely gathering of station hand, storekeeper, garage mechanic, schoolteacher, baker, many with ribbons on their lapels.

There is no music for their march, no bugle or trumpet or tuba. Just a drum and its tap, tap, tap, to pull tired shoulders back and sagging stomachs tight.

In the cities or out of them, bearing floral wreaths or single blooms, the Australians come to heap their memories at the base of the marble monuments to the Anzac dead.

Rarely are battles celebrated or commemorated by the losers. Rarely is the scything of a nation's youth made an occasion for parades and speeches like those which follow the dawn on Anzac Day. But rarely has a nation been dealt a blow so shockingly cold and brutal that its effects linger for years afterwards. Oh, there had been Australian contingents to other wars – in the Sudan, against the Boers. But these were shiny, flag-waving affairs, serious only to those who were killed. These were wars of bravura, with music hall songs and red uniform jackets and formation advances to the rolling of drums.

All the photographs in this chapter were taken on the morning of Anzac Day in Martin Place, Sydney New South Wales.

There was nothing in them to prepare Australians for the coves and cliffs of Gallipoli, from which the waves of black-printed casualty lists swelled and broke on unbelieving minds. And as those waves recoiled from the consciousness of the fledgling nation of less than five million, they took with them the heart and soul of its immediate future – the thinkers and doers, the poets and artisans, the surgeons and singers. That, and each Anzac Day thereafter, offered Australia the realisation that distance and youth alone are no armour against pain.

So Australia began its growing up. A heavily saddened affair, but still a growing up . . . .

We have come now to a point of determination, not unique but new to us, of choosing the way. Like other peoples before us we have won the historical responsibility of freeing, if we are prepared to free, the intellects of newer generations, and sending them on.

As we do this, we shall have to be sure that our histories, legends and all the anecdotes of our journey fall into proper perspective and proportion. The present, after all, is only the sum of all our past, and we should try to get that right before we go on future ways as yet but poorly signposted. We deceive ourselves if we frame and preserve only the daguerreotyped pictures of our achievement.

The Australia of *now*, which is what we are concerned with, is the fruit of much human aspiration and striving, of an uninterrupted and probably interminable conflict with a land which makes very few concessions.

This has left us as a people in a curiously enthralled bondage to the brown sea-girt continent which still scales us down to human puniness, and still resists. This is no docile, submissive mistress. We seldom boast when we are in her presence, and keep our swagger for when we are away.

The long effort of the accumulated past, the stamp and seal of our nationhood, you might say, we have tried to fix and symbolise on an experience of war that occurred half a world away and half a century ago. Anzac is the closest we have ever come to a national-religious feeling, to finding a symbol of the human, perhaps even of the particularly Australian spirit.

The fact is that we are rare as a people in that there are no great victories peculiarly our own which we can elevate as banners. There is no vivid single cause of struggle–save, again, the single cause and struggle of commitment to the land itself. And since we have frowned on the institution of heroes, there are no Great Men to adorn our icons. Cook? Phillip? Flinders? Macquarie? These are worthy men, but figures in a history, occurring when we were the recipients of distant news of the Nelsons and Wellingtons and Napoleons. The explorers? But these are strange sad figures out of dreams, surrealist images in bizarre settings, finally conquered themselves by what they tried to conquer. No figure in this gigantic landscape grows superhuman.

One is moved on Anzac Day by the slouch hat passively at rest on a chair beside the march-route, the hat of Billy Hughes, the "Little Digger," Australia's Prime Minister in the First World War, upon which the ageing marchers filing past toss their sprigs of rosemary. And this

waspish and political little Welshman is about as close as we have ever got to a Great Man in the sense I mean. But he belonged to a vanished, chauvinistic time, and was significant only to a particular generation.

The one thing that remains constant, and has remained constant since that January day in 1788, is the challenge of this country. It is the most exciting thing about Australia. There is still so much to be done.

Here, in a world where so many have come to fear the beginning of the end, Australia has come only to the end of the beginning. The smell of imminence, of things yet to happen, pervades the air as insistently as that unforgettable and indescribably faint odour of the bush, of smoke and hot sun on tree bark, and it drifts in even to the edges of the cities when the sea-salt is not on the wind. The sea, the bush, and the land: this is Australia, and perhaps this is the true hero and image-maker, the huge unconquered land itself.

Perhaps deep down inside the Australian people there lies the hard core of a kind of inarticulate paganism, which mutely worships the old, capricious gods of the earth itself, and the grace and penance of seasons good and bad. We have had our share of both since 1788. We are still in tenancy and so far we have not done badly.

What is important, finally, is that we are here, and we have dug in, and we are going on.

Photographic Data

I bought for this assignment nine Nikon bodies (six Nikon F, two Nikonos, one Nikkormat FT), five motor drive units (four F-36 and one F-250), and thirty Nikkor lenses ranging from the 8mm "Fisheye" to the 1,200mm Tele-Nikkor. Among the lenses ordered were two 21mm, three 28mm, three 105mm, and two of the superb 200mm telephotos.

While I normally carry only two camera bodies plus the 28mm, 55mm Micro-Nikkor, 105mm, and 200mm lenses, and do more than 90% of my work with this simple package, I knew that I would be faced with picture situations where the specialised lenses and motor drive units would be invaluable. At the project's end, nearly every item in the entire Nikon System had been used in obtaining this coverage.

Wherever the Nikkormat FT camera was used, and it became my standard camera towards the project's end, the metering of the picture situation was done with the camera's built-in CDS system. With the Nikon F, I used either the Photomic-T unit or a Lunasix meter.

During the 24 months of active photography, from one end of Australia to the other, the equipment performed faultlessly.

Personal note:

The United Kingdom edition of this book is dedicated to Dr Melville Bell Grosvenor and the staff of the National Geographic Magazine, an organization with which I had the pleasure of spending three rewarding years. I would like to expand this to include the names of Jim Godbold, Robert Gilka, Bill Garrett, and Lee Battaglia, men who freely gave of their rich talents and of their friendship.

Twelve years ago, on graduation from Ohio University, I began a professional association with Howard Chapnick of Black Star Publishing Co. in New York. In the world of photography, Howard Chapnick's friendship is one I value highly, and I would like to thank him for his continued support and for his many kindnesses.

ROBERT B. GOODMAN

Abbreviations to be used for film—

KR II	Kodachrome II
KX	Kodachrome X
EX	Ektachrome X
EH	High Speed Ektachrome
EHB	High Speed Ektachrome Type B
CX	Kodacolor X
CPS	Ektacolor S Professional

Chapter One

(*page 25*) The photograph of the drought-stricken ram had to convey a mocking "life after death" quality. Bright sunlight, KR II film, Nikkormat FT, 28mm Auto-Nikkor lens.

(*pages 26-27*) An aerial photograph; EX film was used for maximum colour saturation in the weak but strongly directional early morning sunlight. Nikkormat FT, 28mm lens.

(*pages 28-29*) (LEFT) 28 mm lens on Nikkormat FT, early morning aerial photograph of the Olgas. KR II film.
(RIGHT) A photograph of a kangaroo in full flight was essential for the book. Getting up before dawn, one Land Rover and driver, a Nikon F, motor drive, EX film, and the 105mm lens all helped. The kangaroos spotted in the early morning sunlight were circled at high speed over rough paddocks in the Land Rover. Between and during the spine-shattering bumps four rolls were exposed. The kangaroos had a far easier time of it, only getting winded in the process. Backlighted and 1½ stops open from front-lighted meter reading gave me a maximum possible shutter speed of 1/250th of a second, still allowing a slightly blurred background.

(*pages 30-31*) On detail photographs of the land I used the 55mm Micro-Nikkor and either EX film for high colour saturation or KR II film depending on the light. All photographs: Nikon F.

(*pages 32-33*) (LEFT) This photograph came by pure chance. Climbing Ayers Rock long after sunset, I saw some two miles away a small rain squall moving slowly across the land. Fortunately I had a heavy tripod along. Metering the darkening sky with my Lunasix, I programmed an exposure of three minutes and following a flash of lightning waited as long as my nerves allowed before opening the shutter. In this way seven proper exposures were made, the longest being five minutes, and during five of the seven exposures there was a flash of lightning. KR II film, Nikon F with the 55mm Micro-Nikkor.

(*pages 34-35*) There is little one can do about blue casts on snow except through proper filtration and unfortunately my one UV filter was not enough. Aerial, KR II film and Nikon F with the 55mm Micro-Nikkor.
(RIGHT) On the black boulders, tiny figures and a single green tree make the picture. But a grey day, KR II film, a hand-held Nikon F with the 200mm lens and a slow shutter speed didn't help.

(*pages 36-37*) (LEFT) Getting aerials of the Great Barrier Reef is both difficult and expensive. The Lindeman Island people provided me with a three-engined Drover and with the door removed the picture taking was easy. Almost at cloud level and into the sun, low tide gives a feeling of the reef's edge. Nikon F, KR II film, 28mm lens.
(LEFT CENTRE) At low tide you find hundreds of marine creatures submerged in only a few inches of crystal-clear water. Bright sunlight, KR II film, 55mm Micro-Nikkor and 105mm lenses.
(RIGHT) Low tide on the Great Barrier Reef from the air gives the jewel-like colour and organic pattern visible in one of the inner reef areas. Nikon F, KR II film, 35mm f/2.8 lens.

(*pages 38-39*) (LEFT) Tramping off into a Victorian rainforest at dawn loaded down with cameras and tripod is more fun than it sounds. Between rain-showers EX film gave the rich colour, a heavy tripod, Nikon F and 35mm f/2.8 lens provided the sharpness of image.
(RIGHT) The graceful loops of Queensland's Fitzroy River show the early morning grey-blue light that comes with putting the sun at one's back. Shooting into the sun produced strikingly different pictures. Nikkormat FT camera, 35mm f/2.8 lens, and KR II film.

(*pages 40-41*) (LEFT) EX film, Nikkormat FT and 105mm lens.
(RIGHT) We spent more than an hour photographing the different play of sunshine on the hills as a strong wind pushed low broken cloud across the sky. KR II film, Nikkormat FT with the 55mm Micro-Nikkor lens.

(*pages 42-43*) (LEFT) It happened very quickly. The fire truck was blocked in by other vehicles and the bushfire moved faster than any of us expected. There was time for three fast exposures before I joined the race to a safer position. KR II film, Nikon F and the 28mm lens.
(RIGHT) We reached the aboriginal group well after sunset and hand holding the Nikkormat FT with an 85mm f/1.8 Auto-Nikkor and EH film is all that pulled that picture situation out of the fire.

(*page 44*) A P.C. Nikkor on a Nikon F, a heavy tripod and EX film was the choice here. The P.C. Nikkor gave me the freedom to shift radically the weight of the silhouetted areas without tilting the camera. Lens stopped down for full coverage and the long exposure bracketed.

Chapter Two

(*page 53*) He was a drover with 6,000 head of sheep moving south into New South Wales from Queensland. Nikon F with Photomic-T, 105mm lens and Tri-X film in the failing evening light.

(*pages 54-55*) Don't do it if you want consistent sharpness. Use a tripod. This picture was hand held at a 30th of a second, KR II film, Nikon F and the 105mm Auto-Nikkor lens.

(*pages 56-57*) Out of the corner of my eye I saw the "ringer" come from the Pub, hesitate, and then turn the corner. I turned and shot in a single motion. Tri-X film, Nikon F, 28mm lens.

(*pages 58-59*) (LEFT) The Outback Radio School of the Air. Natural window light. Nikkormat FT, 28mm lens and Tri-X film.
(RIGHT) Aerial photograph of an outback station in heart of the drought country was copied from a KR II original transparency. 55mm Auto Micro-Nikkor lens on Nikon F.

(*pages 60-61*) (LEFT TO RIGHT) 105mm, 105mm and 28mm Auto Nikkor lenses used. Portraits are all natural light on Tri-X developed normally in D-76 mixed 1-1. Camera was the Nikon F.

(*pages 62-63*) (RIGHT) In 1962 I shot a series of aboriginal pictures for the National Geographic at Ernabella Mission Station in South Australia. It was one of those near unavoidable situations where both my guide, and a member of the Mission staff shot their own cameras over my shoulder as I worked. The Mission staff member later received for her picture a silver medal from Kodak and a colour page in LIFE Magazine. My guide, Jeff Findley, owner of Back of Beyond Tours, netted a book jacket for a local publisher and was kind enough to lend me a transparency for this page when we found nothing in our project file to match the simple expression of man blending in and being one with his land.

(*pages 64-65*) (LEFT) During the Brunette Downs Race Meeting, an elderly station hand. 105mm lens, Tri-X, Nikkormat FT.
(RIGHT) Stopping our car for gasoline in Southern Queensland, the sign over the window was irresistible. Hand-held Nikon F, slow shutter speed, Tri-X film.

(*pages 66-67*) I have always found that, to a point, people reflect the emotions that you bring to them. I walked in front of these men, squatted less than three feet away and shot two rolls of film point blank. They were so content within themselves, so full of a very real dignity that while they knew I was photographing them they took no visible notice of the fact. Tri-X film, Nikkormat FT and 28mm lens. Metering through the camera.

(*pages 68-69*) (LEFT) A black and white copy of a KR II original taken with a Nikkormat FT, 105mm Auto-Nikkor lens on Tri-X film.
(RIGHT) The roof of a parked truck for elevation, Nikkormat FT, 50mm f/2 lens and Tri-X film.

(*pages 70-71*) (LEFT) A black and white copy of a KR II original. $1\frac{1}{4}$ stops open from direct sunlight reading, Nikon F and the 105mm lens.
(RIGHT) A patch of sunlight near the finish line, EH film, a 4-X neutral density filter, the 500mm f/5 Catadioptric Mirror Reflex lens, and a Nikon F were used for the shot. No motor drive.

(*page 72*) The only difficulty was getting the enormous range of sunlight and shadow on to film. Tri-X, Nikon F and the 28mm lens.

Chapter Three

(*page 85*) The telephoto is for me the obvious answer. This was the 105mm Auto-Nikkor on a Nikkormat FT with Tri-X film and bright sunlight.

(*pages 86-87*) (LEFT) EX aerial film of a Western Sydney suburb, Nikon F and the 50mm f/2 Auto-Nikkor lens.
(RIGHT) Nikon F, KR II film, 105mm lens.

(*pages 88-89*) (LEFT) The 200mm lens compressed this busy street scene. The reproduction is part of an 18x24 inch blow-up of the Tri-X original. Nikkormat body.
(RIGHT) The sign was by the side of the road just outside Surfer's Paradise in Queensland. Nikkormat FT, 105mm lens, Tri-X film.

(*pages 90-91*) (LEFT) I had only Kodachrome in the camera for this aerial. Nikkormat FT and the 105mm lens. Tri-X copy using the 135mm short mount Nikkor and bellows unit.

(RIGHT) The Moomba festival each year in Melbourne draws huge crowds to see the big parade. The 135mm lens, Nikon F, Tri-X film.

(*pages 92-93*) Soft sunlight, Nikon F, 28mm lens, Tri-X film. Stopping down and using the preview button helped make this picture.

(*pages 94-95*) (LEFT) Queensland week-end playground. KR II film, Nikkormat FT camera and 55mm Micro-Nikkor lens.
(CENTRE) Nikkormat FT, CPS film, 105mm lens.
(RIGHT) Fastidious Australian homeowner. Nikkormat FT 50mm f/2 Auto-Nikkor, CPS film.

(*pages 96-97*) (LEFT) Tennis coach. Tri-X film, Nikkormat FT, 105mm lens.
(RIGHT UPPER) Aerial of Canberra, KR II film, Nikon F, 35mm f/2.8 Auto-Nikkor.
(RIGHT LOWER) Garden party at Government House, Canberra, shot from balcony. CPS film, 35mm f/2.8 lens and Nikon F.

(*pages 98-99*) (LEFT) Natural light was the final choice even though it meant one-second exposures and unavoidable movement in the picture. Tri-X film, tripod mounted Nikon F with the mirror locked up and the 21mm wide-angle.
(RIGHT) At a football game in Western Australia, the 200mm Auto-Nikkor lens, Nikkormat FT, Tri-X film, and bright sunlight got the picture.

(*pages 100-101*) (LEFT) The young Sydney surf and beach enthusiast was photographed with the Nikon F, 200mm lens, and Tri-X film.
(RIGHT) The policeman kept telling me to get my tripod out of the way of the automobiles and I finally did *after* I got the picture. 28mm Auto-Nikkor, Nikon F on Tripod, Tri-X film. The exposure was the time between warnings by the policeman.

(*pages 102-103*) (LEFT, CENTRE, RIGHT) Foyer and marquee lighting and all the crush of an opening night is made to order for the Nikkormat FT with a 28mm lens in place. Tri-X and D76 films more often than not get the images for me.

(*page 104*) It is mandatory in Australia that a single-engine airplane be on the ground a few short minutes after sunset. So getting an aerial photograph of the sun setting over Sydney's harbour is rather like a rendezvous in space exercise. We had minutes to get into position at the right altitude while the sun dropped relentlessly toward the horizon. The Nikkormat FT and a 35mm lens, EX film.

Chapter Four

(*page 113*) Detail of the crumbling wall of a convict-built penitentiary at Port Arthur, Tasmania, demanded extreme sharpness. Tripod-mounted Nikon F with the 55mm Auto-Micro-Nikkor lens in place. Exposure on Tri-X was for thinnest possible full range negative.

(*pages 114-115*) (LEFT) We found the Chinese burial shrine in a wooded field outside Cooktown, Queensland. I used a number of lenses trying for the effect of a suddenly discovered old tomb looming up out of a wood. The 500mm f/5 Mirror Reflex lens did the trick with its single plane of focus. Hand held on KR II film, Nikon F.

(RIGHT) Old Mrs Schearing in her gold rush days' mud and burlap home in Hill End, N.S.W. There was no electricity in the house. We strung a cable over 100 yards to bring in power for a single quartz iodine 1,000 watt flood bounced in a dark corner of the room. Tripod mounted Nikon F, 28mm lens and Tri-X film.

(*pages 116-117*) The people of the inland city of Bathurst, N.S.W., spent twelve months preparing for their 150th birthday celebration, in costume a faultless re-creation of their colonial past. Nikon F Photomic-T, EH film, and the 28mm Auto-Nikkor lens for all three pictures.

(*pages 118-119*) (LEFT) It was a South Australian German community "shooting festival." Grab-shot, zone focused Nikon F, 28mm lens, Tri-X.
(RIGHT) Same equipment, but this situation required me to career around the dance floor shooting each time they became back-lighted.

(*pages 120-121*) (LEFT) Backlighting in colour with no fill-in light or reflector demanded extensive exposure bracketing. Low angle, Nikon F, 28mm lens, EH film.
(RIGHT) Yugoslav community church picnic and pig roast shot from high in the roof beams of the cooking shed. Heat, smoke and grease were nearly unbearable. Hand-held and bounced M3-B flashbulb gave some fill-in. Nikon F, EX film and 28mm lens.

(*pages 122-123*) (LEFT) The Greek passenger ship had just docked. A 600mm Tele-Nikkor, Nikon F, and heavy tripod brought the passengers waiting to disembark up close. Tri-X film.
(RIGHT) Hand-held 300mm Auto-Nikkor telephoto of Sydney street scene during a Royal visit. Nikkormat FT camera, CPS film, reproduction was from an Ektacolor master print.

(*pages 124-125*) One picture that was essential for this chapter required extremely long telephoto photography. I wanted to see the range of expressions on the faces of migrants lining the railings of a ship being docked at a Sydney pier. I had to shoot into the light and into the shadows of the ship's superstructure. Nikon F, 1,200mm Tele-Nikkor, and Tri-X film.

(*pages 126-127*) (LEFT AND RIGHT) Both pictures were grab-shots with the 28mm lens on a Nikkormat FT, Tri-X film. The situation was the reunion of a Greek family after a ten-year separation.

(*pages 128-129*) (LEFT) Yugoslav migrant family at a country picnic noticed me shooting pictures of them from quite a distance away and posed with delightful self-consciousness. Nikon F, 200mm lens, Tri-X film.
(RIGHT) A Scots lassie at an annual Highland Games in Adelaide, South Australia. Nikkormat FT, 105mm lens, Tri-X film.

(*pages 130-131*) (LEFT) Driving around Rockhampton, Queensland, I shot through my own windscreen, Nikon F, 105mm lens, Tri-X film.
(RIGHT) Australian cowboys at a rodeo in Queensland and a strangely authentic Indian teepee I found abandoned in a field alongside a

Queensland highway. Both are with the Nikkormat FT with 200mm Auto-Nikkor. Film was CPS, black and white prints on Panalure paper.

(*page 132*) Strongly directional window light caught a Thai Colombo Plan graduate student in discussion with his professor. Tri-X film and the 28mm lens on the Nikkormat FT.

Chapter Five

(*page 141*) The problem was to show somehow the size and power of the big machinery the Australian now uses in his battle with the land. A hand-held Nikkormat FT, the 300mm lens and tight cropping has the big machine moving through and out of the picture's right edge. Tri-X.

(*pages 142-143*) These men were gathering unused railway ties at King Bay, Western Australia. A grab-shot with the Nikkormat FT, 28mm pre-focused, and Tri-X film.

(*pages 144-145*) Running in with the 28mm on a Nikkormat FT body there was time for only six exposures before the action was over. The darkness of the picture, its wide-angled foreshortening, the relative size of the man, all help to exaggerate the sense of "scale." Tri-X film.

(*pages 146-147*) (LEFT) Aerials are easy. All you need is a bit of luck with the weather, a pilot who knows where you want to go and can take you there, and a rather cavalier attitude about money. This last because what you need more than anything is a pig-headed stubbornness not to come down, no matter how long it takes, until you've seen and shot the picture you went up to get. KR II film, 55mm Micro-Nikkor on a Nikon F body, exposure by meter.

(RIGHT UPPER) Looking down on irrigated orange trees. 105mm lens, Nikkormat FT, EX film.

(RIGHT LOWER) 28mm lens on a Nikkormat FT, KR II film, metered through the camera system.

(*pages 148-149*) (LEFT) On each circle of the rice paddies I could manage only three exposures with the sun in the most dramatic back-light position. Some thirty passes were made for this picture. Tri-X film 1/1000th of a second at f/22 the 105mm lens and a Nikon F body.

(RIGHT) The problem with the picture of bulk loading the Russian grain carrier was simply to catch the wave-like pulses of wheat being ejected from the mouth of the bulk loader. Various shutter speeds were used, a 500th doing the trick. Tri-X film, 28mm lens and a Nikon F.

(*pages 150-151*) (LEFT) I had only one day to shoot pictures of cotton. The puffy white clouds were a lucky bonus. The picture itself was another grab-shot, KR II film, 28mm lens on a Nikon F.

(RIGHT) Aerial of wheat-field patterns, Darling Downs region of south Queensland, Nikon F, EX film, 35mm 2.8 lens.

(*pages 152-153*) (LEFT AND RIGHT) The pictures are interdependent, one qualifying in strongly human terms the action of making the sandy land stable enough to grow eucalypts and other soil-binding flora. 35mm 2.8 lens on left, Micro-Nikkor on right, Nikkormat FT body and Tri-X.

(*pages 154-155*) (LEFT) The north-west of Australia is big country and shooting the geological survey team from a distance helps put things in a more accurate perspective. Nikkormat FT body, 35mm 2.8 lens and Tri-X film.

(RIGHT) A supportive close-up, same technical data as picture opposite.

(*pages 156-157*) (LEFT AND RIGHT) Aerial is with the Nikkormat FT, Micro-Nikkor and Tri-X film. Shovel loading ore is shot with same camera and film but with the 28mm lens.

(*pages 158-159*) (LEFT) The oil men were shot with a 55mm Micro-Nikkor and Nikkormat FT body, Tri-X film.

(RIGHT) Aerial from helicopter with a motor-driven Nikon F body, 21mm lens, Tri-X film, fired by remote control.

(*page 160*) The face of the oil "roughneck" was shot with the 105mm lens, Tri-X film, and a Nikkormat FT body.

Chapter Six

(*page 169*) In this one it was the backlighting on the chain links, the heavy metal grippers for the logs, and the circular sawblades themselves, that made the picture for me. 105mm lens, Nikon F body and Tri-X film, guessed exposure.

(*pages 170-171*) The big sky is another "scale" photograph, the sky emphasising the hot emptiness of the place. Tri-X film, 55mm Micro-Nikkor, Nikkormat FT body.

(*pages 172-173*) (LEFT AND RIGHT) The detail picture on the left was taken in natural light, with a Nikkormat FT and 28mm lens, Tri-X film. The aerial shot of sheep was from 105mm, Nikon F, KR II original, copied on 35mm Tri-X film.

(*pages 174-175*) (LEFT) Worker in carpet-making section of plant photographed through the warp (or woof) of a red carpet being woven. EH film, 105mm lens and Nikkormat FT body.

(BELOW) Rolls of wool felt in manufacture. Nikkormat FT, 55mm Micro-Nikkor, EX film.

(*pages 176-177*) (LEFT) The swirling dust created a constantly changing backdrop to the men working the timber stack. Nikkormat FT, 28mm lens, Tri-X film.

(RIGHT) In the paper mill, 28mm lens, Nikkormat FT body, Tri-X film.

(*pages 178-179*) (LEFT) While waiting for another picture, I grabbed a few quick shots of bars of aluminium being shoved into an alloying furnace. The Nikkormat FT took care of the exposure problems, 28mm lens and EH film.

(RIGHT) Basic Oxygen System furnace at Newcastle, N.S.W. To me the drama of steelmaking is so great that it's almost impossible to miss. The Nikkormat FT made the exposure problem simple from 40 yards away. EH film and the 105mm and 200mm lenses on heavy tripod.

(*pages 180-181*) (LEFT) Two of the three portraits were photographed in natural light, the third, of Sir Ian Potter, was done with a hand-held quartz iodine 1,000 watt flood bounced off the ceiling. I often prefer the dramatic quality of the 28mm lens for portraiture. Nikkormat FT and Tri-X film.

(RIGHT) Looking down the nose of a Boeing 707 in workshop for major overhaul and repainting. 200mm lens and Nikon F body, metered by hand, KR II film.

(*pages 182-183*) (LEFT) Production line from high ladder. Natural light EH film, 50mm f/1.4 and Nikkormat FT.

(RIGHT) Bright sun, straightforward shot for the record, Nikkormat FT, 28mm lens and KR II film.

(*page 184*) Nikkormat FT, 55mm Micro-Nikkor, KR II film, and a "smidgen" of backlighting.

Chapter Seven

(*page 193*) I have always used the fisheye lens with reservations. But standing in the centre of the giant "dish" of the Parkes radio-telescope there was only one lens for the job. KR II film, Nikon F, bright sunlight.

(*pages 194-195*) Scale became the major visual problem here. The radio-telescope is so huge that it overwhelms normal objects. Using two small walkie-talkies I asked the engineer controlling the telescope to steer it into the most dramatic position relative to the setting sun and the telephone pole at its base. From the roof of our 4-wheel-drive Scout, a heavy tripod, 200mm lens, KR II film, and a Nikon F got the picture.

(*pages 196-197*) (LEFT) Sir Macfarlane Burnet's laboratory had almost perfect window light. 85mm 1.8 on a Nikkormat FT and EX film.

(RIGHT) EX film and the Micro-Nikkor for the top picture and a 28mm lens for the bottom shot. Nikkormat FT for both and natural window light.

(*pages 198-199*) (LEFT) Dr Bennetts worked all his life to make the land of Western Australia productive. The portrait was the simplest of settings, window light, 105mm lens on the Nikkormat FT, Tri-X film.

(RIGHT) 28mm lens on the Nikkormat FT, natural room lighting and Tri-X film.

(*pages 200-201*) (LEFT) Most of my close-up picture needs fall well within the range of the Micro-Nikkor and its extension "M" ring. The hand-held test tube was lighted by the late afternoon sun. Nikkormat FT, KR II film.

(RIGHT) Record picture of a man in a working situation. Nikkormat FT, 28mm lens, Tri-X film.

(*pages 202-203*) Shooting directly into late afternoon sunlight with the deeply shielded Micro-Nikkor gave us the picture while the Nikkormat FT gave the exposure, Tri-X film.

(*pages 204-205*) (LEFT) Technicians awaiting final results from the computor at Lucas Heights. Hand-held bounced 1,000 watt flood, Nikkormat FT, 28mm lens, Tri-X film.

(RIGHT) Shooting through a research test apparatus filled with alcohol, natural light, tripod, EX film, Nikkormat FT and 105mm lens.

(*pages 206-207*) (LEFT) Missile telemetry-tracking antennae from a low angle, 28mm lens, Nikkormat FT body, Tri-X film.

(RIGHT) Short step-ladder, 35mm 2.8, Nikkormat FT body, Tri-X film.

(*page 208*) When all was said and done we had the usual few seconds to get this shot. Weeks prior to the launching I assembled the gear for the close-up shots; a 250 exp. motor drive, heavy duty battery and relay box, a 135mm 3.5 lens, and heavy duty mounting brackets. This unit was to be mounted in the open within a few hundred yards of the launch complex. Electrically wired into the rocket's firing system, our camera loaded with Ektacolor S Professional negative colour film would begin firing 7 seconds before lift-off. A rocket malfunction and the insurance company would have owned a well-fried Nikon F. To cover ourselves photographically, I stationed myself 2½ miles from the launch point with the big 1,000mm mirror lens on a standard F-36 Nikon. Half an hour's delay caused heat waves to build up, softening the image, and then the rocket lifted off. Both cameras functioned perfectly, but it was the 2½ mile distant sequence that gave the rocket its relationship to the Australian land, a quality important to us editorially.

Chapter Eight

(*page 217*) Gallery visitors, Nikon F, 85mm 1.8 lens, EH film and natural daylight. Black and white copy of the original.

(*pages 218-219*) There were half a dozen frames left over from the shooting session with painter Russell Drysdale. On a whim I asked his wife to join us so that I could run off the roll and give them the double portrait for their own use. EX film, 35mm f/2 lens, natural window light, Nikkormat FT.

(*pages 220-221*) (LEFT) 28mm lens, Nikkormat FT, Tri-X film and a long exposure from tripod for this painting class.
(RIGHT) Again using natural window light, this time with the 85mm 1.8 lens, Tri-X film in the Nikkormat FT body.

(*pages 222-223*) (LEFT AND RIGHT) Both pictures are from the Nikkormat FT, 105mm lens using Tri-X film in natural light.

(*pages 224-225*) (LEFT UPPER) Children's performance, Sydney Symphony Orchestra, from the wings, Tri-X film, natural light, Nikkormat FT and the 105mm 2.5 lens.
(LEFT LOWER) Australian composer Peter Sculthorpe, 50mm f/2 lens, Nikon F, Tri-X film.
(RIGHT) Ballerina Kathleen Gorham during rehearsal of *Yugen*, very low stage lighting, 50mm 1.4 lens, Nikon F, Tri-X film.

(*pages 226-227*) (LEFT) During a rehearsal in the ABC studios in Sydney, Bobby Helpmann's reactions to the actors he was working with provided me with a fast roll of CPS exposures, hand held 1/8th of a second braced against a wall with the 85mm 1.8 lens on a Nikkormat FT.
(RIGHT) During a performance and shot from the wings, the bird-costumed dancer for an instant blocked out the spotlights. EH film, 105mm 2.5 lens, Nikon F, guessed exposure.

(*pages 228-229*) (LEFT) Like the Drysdale picture, I started off on the wrong foot trying to photograph only the poet herself. Judith Wright and her husband were very much married and so we sat and talked and I shot intermittently and so the picture. 28mm lens, Nikkormat FT, Tri-X film and natural light.
(RIGHT) Mary Durack wrote a great Australian saga of the land called *Kings in Grass Castles*. 105mm lens, Nikkormat FT, KR II film.

(*pages 230-231*) (LEFT) The studio was very small, the light wonderfully plastic from the glass doors that opened ceiling to floor. Strongly directional, it emphasised the surface, shape and mass of the clay pot. Nikkormat FT, 28mm lens and KR II film.
(RIGHT) A uni-pod, the 500mm mirror telephoto, and a 1/8th of a second exposure with the Nikon F. Correct exposure was anyone's guess.

(*page 232*) Late evening sun, EX film, and a 500mm lens shot from inverted tripod centre section, camera and lens only inches from the water.

Chapter Nine

(*page 241*) The relay-box, battery pack, 21mm lens, tripod, and Nikon F kept me out of danger. EX film, bright sunlight.

(*pages 242-243*) (LEFT) Young sailor, 105mm lens, Nikon F, CPS film, reproduction from an Ektacolor print.
(LEFT CENTRE) Shooting from a following boat directly into the sun. KR II film, Nikkormat FT, 135mm 3.5 lens.
(RIGHT) The high diving platform gave me the viewpoint, the Nikon F, motor drive and 50mm 1.4 lens gave me the picture.

(*pages 244-245*) (LEFT) EX film for dark rainy afternoon, Nikon F, 105mm lens, hand held 1/8th of a second exposure.
(RIGHT) It was a problem to avoid disrupting the game. An old chair in the outfield gave me a relatively safe position for hand holding the 500mm mirror lens, Nikon F, pistol grip, Tri-X film, bright sunlight, 4x neutral density filter.

(*pages 246-247*) This is one frame of a sequence of four, the best of two full days of photography. I was using the Nikon F and 500mm mirror lens tripod mounted. KR II film, bright sunlight.

(*pages 248-249*) Provided you have the time and money, there isn't much to this kind of photography. It took three prototype waterproof housings before we got the fourth designed correctly. It took three different sets of experimental radio gear before we found a combination that was utterly reliable. A specially designed surfboard had to be built, a bracket to hold the camera high on its nose. The surf had to be just right, the board rider very experienced. Given all these things I just sat down on the beach and transmitter in hand waited for the surfer to get positioned on a big wave. Then just a flick of the switch started the Nikon F's motor drive going, and the Tri-X film and 21mm lens did the rest.

(*pages 250-251*) (LEFT) The 1,000mm mirror lens, a Nikon F body, and a late afternoon sun gave us the picture on KR II film.
(BELOW) Sunlight, 28mm lens, KRII, Nikkormat FT.

(*pages 252-253*) This was the "gala" day for youngsters on local suburban soccer teams to parade *en masse* in front of their parents and friends. 105mm lens and the Nikon F and both EX and KR II film.

(*pages 254-255*) (LEFT) Jockeys in the waiting area before a big race. Window light, Nikkormat FT and 35mm f/2.8 lens. EH film.
(RIGHT) Both the sign in the picture's centre and the varying dress of the men added up to an editorial comment we felt necessary. Nikkormat FT, 50mm f/1.4 lens, KR II film.

(*pages 256-257*) (LEFT TO RIGHT) Ladies at a Melbourne Cup. This is just stroll and shoot photography best done with the 43-85 zoom lens on a Nikkormat FT. KR II film.

(*pages 258-259*) (LEFT) Rugby is not my game. This particular contest was my first ever, and I followed the other press photographers up and down the sidelines asking questions. Fortunately it was very muddy that day; a 105mm lens and the Nikon F gave me a picture. Tri-X film.
(RIGHT) Australian Rules football is intensely exciting, and difficult to photograph well. An 85-250 zoom, Nikon F, and pistol grip was the equipment, Tri-X the film.

(*pages 260-261*) The game of Australian Rules football keeps the spectators in a near frenzy of emotion. EX film was picked for its intense and exciting colour saturation, particularly in bright sunlight. Nikkormat FT and the 28mm lens.

(*pages 262-263*) I saw this picture building from thirty yards away. The sun streaming through an opening between the stands, the athletes on the raised platform, photographers jockeying for position, these were all the ingredients. Nikon F, 28mm lens, CPS film, guessed exposure, and reproduction from an Ektacolor print.

Chapter Ten

(*pages 277-284*) All photographs with the exception of the second picture in this chapter were taken with the Nikon F, 28mm lens and Tri-X film. The second picture called for the 200mm telephoto with the camera tripod mounted.

Darkroom Data

From the standpoint of my own available darkroom time I owe much of the project's success to the Durst M-35 Micromat enlarger which allowed me to turn out 300 to 400 work prints in a single day. The auto-focus speed and precision of the M-35 allowed the book's designer and me to work layout variations on the enlarger's baseboard, projecting colour slides directly on to a white layout sheet.

All colour internegatives were made using a Durst D659 enlarger, and master colour and black and white prints were produced on Durst 184, 3s colour and M35 Micromat enlargers. Colour separations for the six and two colour offset plates used in reproducing the photographs used in this book were made on a Durst G139 enlarger using a Staub Xenon impulse light source.

Map Data

Size

Australia is approximately 2,500 miles from east to west and 2,000 miles from north to south, covering 2,967,741 square miles of which 1,147,622 are in the tropics. It is more than half as large again as Europe (excluding Russia) and approximately equal in size to the United States of America (excluding Alaska).
Areas of the six Australian States are: New South Wales, 309,433 square miles; Victoria, 87,884; Queensland, 667,000; South Australia, 380,070; Western Australia, 975,920; and Tasmania, 26,215. The Northern Territory covers 520,280 square miles and the Australian Capital Territory 939 square miles.

Population

The population of Australia reached 11,544,691 on 30 June, 1966. Population distribution revealed by the census of 1961 was: urban metropolitan, 56.12 per cent; urban provincial, 25.82 per cent; rural, 17.82 per cent; and migratory, 0.24 per cent.
Density of population over the entire continent is 3.9 persons to the square mile. This low figure is due to the fact that about a third of the continent is at present uninhabitable, and in another third the rainfall is much too low to permit close settlement. Density comparison with other countries is: Europe (excluding Russia), 225; Netherlands, 897; Belgium, 780; Germany, 563; Britain, 562; Asia (excluding Russia), 165; U.S.A., 51; Russia, 25; and Canada, 5.

The population of the States on June 30, 1966:

New South Wales	4,235,030
Victoria	3,217,832
Queensland	1,661,240
South Australia	1,090,723
Western Australia	835,570
Tasmania	371,217
Australian Capital Territory	95,913
Northern Territory	37,166

The population of capital cities on June 30, 1966:

Sydney	2,444,735
Melbourne	2,108,499
Brisbane	719,140
Adelaide	726,930
Perth	499,494
Hobart	119,415
Canberra	92,199
Darwin	20,261

Figures quoted above are the latest available.

Location

Australia lies south-east of Asia, between the Indian and Pacific Oceans. Perth (Western Australia) is 3,121 miles from Colombo, 4,951 from Cape Town, South Africa, and 9,514 from London. Sydney is 6,456 miles from San Francisco, 3,768 from Singapore and 10,590 air miles from London.

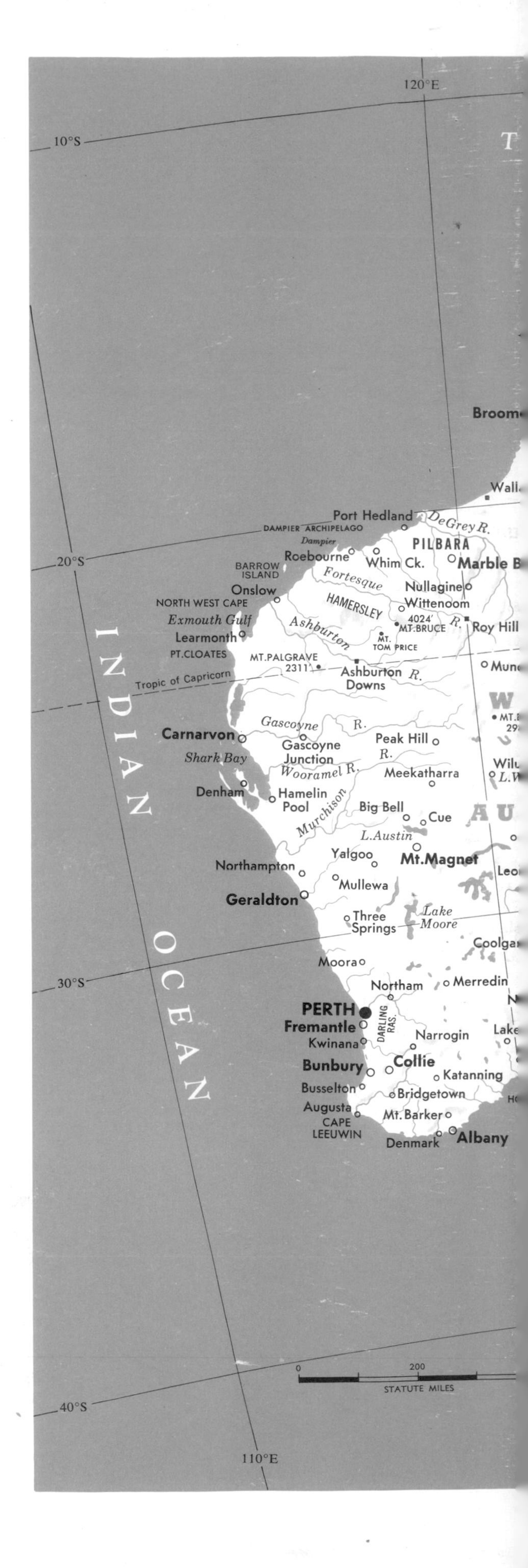

ARAFURA SEA
TORRES STRAIT
CORAL SEA
SOUTH PACIFIC OCEAN
TASMAN SEA
GREAT AUSTRALIAN BIGHT
GULF OF CARPENTARIA
130°E
140°E
150°E
160°E
10°S
20°S
30°S
40°S
Tropic of Capricorn
NORTHERN TERRITORY
QUEENSLAND
SOUTH AUSTRALIA
N. S. W.
VICTORIA
TASMANIA
A.C.T.
DARWIN
BRISBANE
SYDNEY
CANBERRA
MELBOURNE
ADELAIDE
HOBART
MELVILLE ISLAND
BATHURST ISLAND
Van Diemen Gulf
Beagle Gulf
Rum Jungle
Adelaide River
Pine Creek
Edith River
Katherine
Anson Bay
Daly R.
ARNHEM LAND
WESSEL IS.
CAPE ARNHEM
GROOTE EYLANDT
Joseph Bonaparte Gulf
KIMBERLEY
Wyndham
Ivanhoe
Kununurra
MT.HANN 2800'
Drysdale R.
KING LEOPOLD RAS.
Victoria R.
Mataranka
Roper R.
Larrimah
Daly Waters
Victoria River Downs
Borroloola
Limmen Bight
VANDERLIN I.
MORNINGTON ISLAND
Newcastle Waters
Elliott
Lake Woods
Powell Creek
Wave Hill
Inverway
Turkey Creek
Ord R.
Halls Creek
Camballin
Fitzroy Crossing
Fitzroy
Christmas Creek
Margaret River
BARKLY TABLELAND
Brunette Downs
Tennant Creek
Burketown
Karumba
Normanton
Leichhardt R.
Flinders R.
Camooweal
SANDY
The Granites
Wauchope
Hatches Creek
Lake Mackay
CENTRAL MT.STEWART
Barrow Creek
Tea Tree Well
Aileron
Sandover R.
Urandangie
MT.LEISLER 3300'
MT.ZEIL 4955'
Alice Springs
MACDONNELL RAS.
KRICHAUFF RA.
Lake Disappointment
L. Hopkins
Lake Amadeus
Angas Downs
Todd R.
Finke R.
Finke
SIMPSON DESERT
MT.OLGA 3419'
Ayers Rock
Kulgera
GIBSONS DESERT
MUSGRAVE RAS.
Ernabella Mission Sta.
MT. WOODROFFE 4970'
Abminga
GREAT VICTORIA DESERT
Oodnadatta
The Warburton
Goyder Lagoon
STURTS STONY DESERT
Cooper Creek
LAKE EYRE
Coober Pedy
Maralinga
NULLARBOR PLAIN
Cook
Forrest
Madura
Eucla
Balladonia
CAPE ARID
Kingoonya
Marree
Witchelina
Farina
L. Torrens
Andamooka
Leigh Creek
Woomera
L. Gairdner
Ceduna
Port Augusta
FLINDERS RAS.
Quorn
Radium Hill
Minnipa
Whyalla
Kimba
Cleve
EYRE PENIN.
Spencer Gulf
Port Pirie
Peterborough
Port Lincoln
Clare
BAROSSA VALLEY
Gawler
Hahndorf
Murray Bridge
Renmark
Kingscote
KANGAROO ISLAND
Innamincka
L. Blanche
Milparinka
L. Callabonna
L. Frome
Broken Hill
Wilcannia
Menindee
Darling R.
Wentworth
Mildura
Murray R.
Swan Hill
Warracknabeal
Horsham
Naracoorte
Hamilton
Mt.Gambier
Warrnambool
Colac
Geelong
Ballarat
Bendigo
Shepparton
Ferntree Gully
Morwell
WILSON'S PROMONTORY
KING ISLAND
Bass Strait
FLINDERS ISLAND
Burnie
Devonport
Bell Bay
Launceston
Queenstown
Swansea
Port Arthur
Thursday Island
CAPE YORK
CAPE GRENVILLE
Weipa
Iron Range
CAPE DIRECTION
Albatross Bay
CAPE YORK PENINSULA
Coen
CAPE MELVILLE
CAPE FLATTERY
Mitchell River
Mitchell R.
Laura
Palmer R.
Cooktown
BLACK MTNS.
THE GREAT BARRIER REEF
Delta Downs
Cairns
Atherton
Innisfail
Tully
Georgetown
Croydon
HINCHINBROOK I.
Ingham
Townsville
Burdekin R.
Ayr
Charters Towers
Hayman Island
WHITSUNDAY I.
LINDEMAN I.
Bowen
Proserpine
Brampton Island
Mt.Isa
Cloncurry
Mary Kathleen
Julia Creek
Richmond
Hughenden
Dajarra
Georgina R.
Boulia
Winton
Muttaburra
Diamantina R.
Mackay
GREAT DIVIDING RANGE
Longreach
Thomson R.
Clermont
CAPE MANIFOLD
Fitzroy R.
Rockhampton
Emerald
Alpha
Barcaldine
Mt.Morgan
CURTIS I.
Gladstone
Callide
Thangool
Moura
Jundah
Isisford
Blackall
Windorah
Barcoo R.
L.Philippi
Hay R.
L.Machattie
Birdsville
L.Yamma Yamma
Monto
Bundaberg
Gayndah
FRAZER I.
Maryborough
Quilpie
Charleville
Roma
Mitchell
Gympie
Nambour
Kingaroy
Dalby
Thargomindah
Cunnamulla
St. George
Moonie
Oakey
Toowoomba
MT. TAMBORINE
Southport
Coolangatta
Warwick
Goondiwindi
Dirranbandi
GREY RANGE
Bulloo R.
Paroo R.
Warrego R.
Hungerford
Collarenebri
Moree
Casino
Lismore
Bourke
Walgett
Inverell
Grafton
Narrabri
Armidale
Coffs Harbour
Coonamble
Nyngan
Cobar
Tamworth
Kempsey
Scone
Taree
Dubbo
Mudgee
Lachlan R.
Parkes
Hill End
Maitland
Orange
Lithgow
Newcastle
Bathurst
BLUE MTS.
Griffith
Murrumbidgee R.
Hay
Wagga Wagga
Narrandera
Deniliquin
Goulburn
Wollongong
Port Kembla
Nowra
Albury
Wangaratta
SNOWY MTS.
MT. KOSCIUSKO 7316'
Cooma
Bega

The concept of this book, to try to define and express the Australians as a people, pictorially and textually, began in the bar of a hotel in Alice Springs, continued in a club at the Adelaide Festival, eventually involved tens of thousands of miles of travel by each of us independently, and finally the discarding of thousands of words of copy and thousands of pictures to try to get to the essence of an image.

We would not have been able to afford the time and expense of such travels over such distances (the search for pictures of "The Wet" in a time of desperate continental drought was a case in point) nor the discriminating wastage of material without the sponsorship of a group of important business organisations dedicated to the simple objective we had in mind – the fair and unpropagandised presentation of the Australian in his unique and many-faceted setting. The essential image, if you like, of a race apart from others.

We should like to thank this consortium of sponsors who, without any strings of publicity attached, and without any rulings on what was to be included and what was to be left out, generously backed the project of *The Australians*. This was public relations at the highest level, and the organisations involved were:
Alcoa of Australia, Ansett Transport Industries, Associated Pulp and Paper Mills, Broken Hill Proprietary, Commonwealth Banking Corporation, Felt & Textiles, IBM Australia, International Harvester, Mutual Life and Citizens Assurance Company, P & O – Orient Lines of Australia, Qantas, H. C. Sleigh Limited.

We should also like to express our thanks to the Australian National Travel Association for co-ordinating the project, and to the innumerable organisations and individuals ranging from the very humble to the highly distinguished, from the station stockman to the Nobel Prize winner, who helped us on the way.

ROBERT B. GOODMAN

GEORGE JOHNSTON

SOUTH ORANGE PUBLIC LIBRARY
3 9507 00059625 3